www.ingramcontent.com/pod-product-compliance
Ingram Content Group UK Ltd.
Pitfield, Milton Keynes, MK11 3LW, UK
UKHW041824200726
13854UKWH00002BA/535

9 781782 011590

[illegible] [illegible] [illegible]

[illegible]

Aliz kalandjai Csodaországban

𐲀𐲖𐲐𐲯 𐲔𐲀𐲖𐲀𐲙𐲇𐲒𐲀𐲐
𐲆𐲛𐲇𐲀𐲛𐲢𐲥𐲁𐲍𐲂𐲀𐲙

Írta

Lewis Carroll

A Hungarian translation
of *Alice's Adventures in Wonderland*
printed in the Old Hungarian Alphabet

ILLUSZTRÁLTA

JOHN TENNIEL

MAGYARRA FORDÍTOTTA

SZILÁGYI ANIKÓ

2016

Kiadja/*Published by* Evertype, 73 Woodgrove, Portlaoise, R32 ENP6, Ireland. *www.evertype.com*.

A mű eredeti címe/*Original title*: *Alice's Adventures in Wonderland*.

Szaklektor/*Advisory editor*: Anna Kőszeghy

Első kiadás/*First edition* 2016.

A könyvhöz tartozó katalógus bejegyzés megtalálható a British Library katalógusában.
A catalogue record for this book is available from the British Library.

ISBN-10 1-78201-159-5
ISBN-13 978-1-78201-159-0

De Vinne Text, Mona Lisa, ENGRAVERS' ROMAN, és Liberty betűtípusból szedte Michael Everson.
Typeset in De Vinne Text, Mona Lisa, ENGRAVERS' ROMAN, *and* Liberty *by* Michael Everson.

Illusztrációk/*Illustrations*: John Tenniel, 1865.

Borító/*Cover*: Michael Everson.

Nyomta/*Printed by* LightningSource.

[illegible] 1935 [illegible][1] [illegible]

[illegible] "the chimneys were shaped like ears and the) roof was thatched with fur" [illegible]

"[illegible]"

[illegible]

[illegible]

[illegible] 1 [illegible] 1970 [illegible] 1935 [illegible] 1974 [illegible] (2010 [illegible]).

[illegible]

> "After such a fall as this, I shall think nothing of tumbling downstairs! How brave they'll all think me at home! Why, I wouldn't say anything about it, even if I fell off the top of the house!" (Which was very likely true.)

[illegible]

[illegible]

[illegible] "March Hare" [illegible]

[illegible] 2009 [illegible]

[illegible]

> First came ten soldiers carrying clubs: these were all shaped like the three gardeners, oblong and flat, with their hands and feet at the corners: next the ten courtiers: these were ornamented all over with diamonds, and walked two and two, as the soldiers did. After these came the royal children: there were ten of them, and the little dears came jumping merrily along hand in hand, in couples: they were all ornamented with hearts. Next came the guests, mostly Kings and Queens, and among them Alice recognized the White Rabbit: it was talking in a hurried nervous manner, smiling at everything that was said, and went by without noticing her. Then followed the Knave of Hearts, carrying the King's crown on a crimson velvet cushion; and, last of all this grand procession, came THE KING AND THE QUEEN OF HEARTS.

[illegible] *clubs* [illegible] *diamonds* [illegible] *spades* [illegible] *hearts* [illegible][2]

---

2 [illegible] -1935 [illegible] -1974 [illegible]

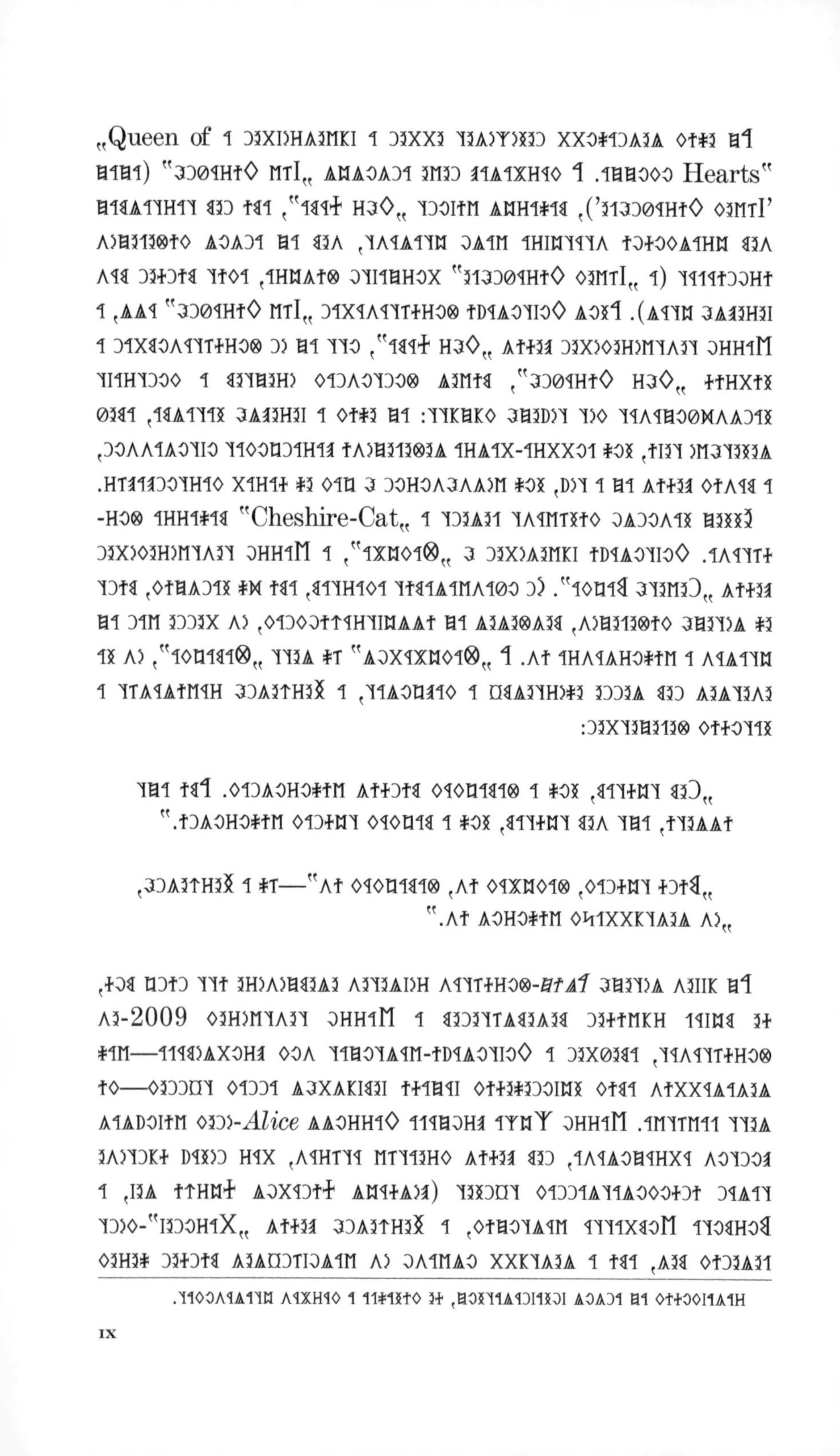

[illegible] „Queen of [illegible] Hearts" [illegible] ('Itmeo [illegible]'), [illegible] („Itmeo [illegible]") [illegible] „Itm [illegible]" [illegible] „Itm [illegible]" [illegible]

[illegible] „Cheshire-Cat" [illegible] „Cimeye [illegible]" [illegible] „Xrhocei"- [illegible]

„[illegible]"

„[illegible]"

[illegible] 2009 [illegible] Alice [illegible]

[illegible]

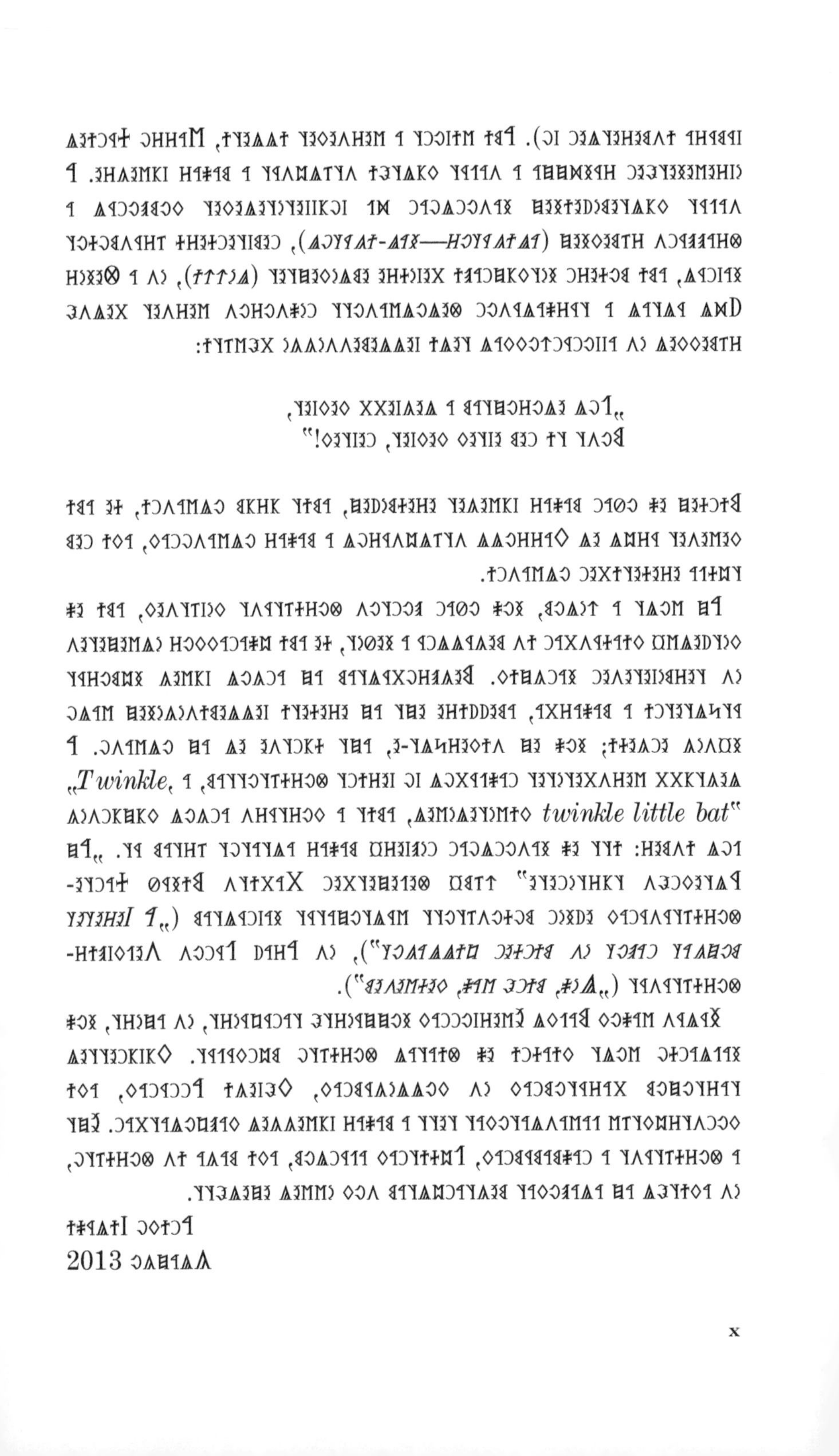

[illegible]

[illegible]

[illegible]

[illegible] „*Twinkle*, [illegible] *twinkle little bat*” [illegible]

[illegible]

[illegible]
[illegible] 2013

ꟻ T ⊗ ꟻ H Λ Ɔ T Λ X T X

Józan Ildikó. [n.d.]. 'Nyelvek poétikája: Alice, Évike, Kosztolányi meg a szakirodalom és a fordítás'. *Filológiai Közlöny* 2010 (3): 213–238.

Carroll, Lewis. 1935. *Évike Tündérországban*. Ford. Kosztolányi Dezső. Budapest: Gergely R.

Carroll, Lewis. 1974. *Alice Csodaországban*. Szerk. Szobotka Tibor. Ford. Kosztolányi Dezső. Budapest: Móra. mek.oszk.hu/00300/00348/html/.

Carroll, Lewis. 2000. 'Alice's Adventures in Wonderland'. In *The Annotated Alice: The Definitive Edition*, szerk. Martin Gardner, 11–127. New York és London: W. W. Norton & Company.

Carroll, Lewis. 2009. *Aliz kalandjai Csodaországban és a tükör másik oldalán*. Ford. Varró Zsuzsa és Varró Dániel. Budapest: Sziget Könyvkiadó.

Foreword

Lewis Carroll is a pen-name: Charles Lutwidge Dodgson was the author's real name and he was lecturer in Mathematics in Christ Church, Oxford. Dodgson began the story on 4 July 1862, when he took a journey in a rowing boat on the river Thames in Oxford together with the Reverend Robinson Duckworth, with Alice Liddell (ten years of age), the daughter of the Dean of Christ Church, and with her two sisters, Lorina (thirteen years of age), and Edith (eight years of age). As is clear from the poem at the beginning of the book, the three girls asked Dodgson for a story and reluctantly at first he began to tell the first version of the story to them. Many half-hidden references are made to the five of them throughout the text of the book itself, which was published finally in 1865.

Growing up in Budapest in the 1990s I found that *Alice* occupied a unique position in children's literature in Hungary. It was a book everyone had heard of but few were actually familiar with. Our knowledge of the characters came primarily from the various film and television adaptations, especially the Disney one, or perhaps from the numerous abridged versions, and only rarely from having read the

original work. The book was certainly well-known as an English children's classic, but had not quite achieved the status of a Hungarian favourite.

I read *Alice* in Hungarian as a child and loved it; later I read it in English and considered myself a fan. The idea of retranslating *Alice's Adventures in Wonderland* first occurred to me when I was skimming through a bilingual edition containing a 1935 Hungarian translation by renowned poet Dezső Kosztolányi.[1] As I got to the end of Chapter VI, where Alice first sees the house of the March Hare, I noticed something peculiar in the translated text. When Carroll's narrator describes the house, we learn that "the chimneys were shaped like ears and the roof was thatched with fur". In the Hungarian this becomes the following:

> "Nem kellett sokáig mennie, egyszer csak ott volt előtte Április Bolondjának a háza. Nyomban sejtette, hogy ez az a ház. A két kéménye sután kétfelé állt, a teteje pedig széllel volt bélelve."
>
> [She did not have far to go, suddenly the house of April's Fool stood before her. She suspected straight away that this was the right house. The two chimneys were pointing clumsily in opposite directions, and the roof was lined with wind.]

1 For simplicity's sake I will refer to this translation as Kosztolányi's, although in reality the version which has been circulating since the 1970s as Kosztolányi's translation is best described as a collaboration. Kosztolányi published his translation under the title *Évike Tündérországban* [Evie in Fairyland] in 1935, but this text was judged as overly "Hungarianized" and was substantially re-edited by Tibor Szobotka before its publication in 1974 as *Alice Csodaországban* [Alice in Wonderland]. The general public is usually completely unaware that what they read as Kosztolányi's *Alice* contains significant changes made by Szobotka (Józan: 11).

"Lined with wind" is a Hungarian idiom meaning 'feather-brained' or 'fidgety', adjectives that certainly apply to the March Hare or, in Kosztolányi's translation, "April's Fool". I still felt that the Hungarian expression was somehow inappropriate. It is a clever attempt, as the humour is retained but the references to the March Hare's animal qualities ("shaped like ears", "thatched with fur") are removed. Why, then, does it seem incongruous in the narrative?

The reason is that here Kosztolányi transfers the absurd to the narrative voice, thereby violating the dynamics of the source text, where the absurd is restricted to the rhetoric of the *characters*. Although a great number of magical events occur throughout Carroll's story, the narrator dutifully recounts them in what seems to be an objective, rational voice. Much of the humour in *Alice* lies in the characters saying or doing absurd things, or magical events occurring, and the narrator commenting on them with dry sarcasm, which highlights the contrast between fantasy and realism. A case in point is the monologue Alice delivers while she is falling down the rabbit-hole—a rather improbable situation—followed by the narrator's remark in brackets:

> "After such a fall as this, I shall think nothing of tumbling downstairs! How brave they'll all think me at home! Why, I wouldn't say anything about it, even if I fell off the top of the house!" (Which was very likely true.)

Awareness of such a key feature of the source text is crucial to a good translation. Kosztolányi's version, although very creative and entertaining, does not conform to contemporary ideas of what a translation should be, because translation norms in the early twentieth century afforded translators much greater liberty than current ones do. Today's readers generally expect closer parity between source and target, which is one of the reasons why a more accurate and up-to-

date translation of *Alice's Adventures in Wonderland* was needed.

An obvious solution to the problem of rendering "the March Hare" in Hungarian, where hares have no connotation of madness, would be translating it as *Május Szamara* ("May's Donkey"), after the saying "April's Fool, May's Donkey". This, however, would be inconsistent with John Tenniel's illustrations depicting a hare. I settled for what I thought was the second best solution: I called him "the April Hare", as this partially retains the reference to madness, perhaps more so than "Pentecostal Hare" in the 2009 translation by Zsuzsa and Dániel Varró.

Another example of the ways in which Kosztolányi's version falls short of modern expectations is the passage describing the court's appearance in the chapter titled "The Queen's Croquet-Ground":

> First came ten soldiers carrying clubs: these were all shaped like the three gardeners, oblong and flat, with their hands and feet at the corners: next the ten courtiers: these were ornamented all over with diamonds, and walked two and two, as the soldiers did. After these came the royal children: there were ten of them, and the little dears came jumping merrily along hand in hand, in couples: they were all ornamented with hearts. Next came the guests, mostly Kings and Queens, and among them Alice recognized the White Rabbit: it was talking in a hurried nervous manner, smiling at everything that was said, and went by without noticing her. Then followed the Knave of Hearts, carrying the King's crown on a crimson velvet cushion; and, last of all this grand procession, came THE KING AND THE QUEEN OF HEARTS.

This paragraph is a real challenge to translate into Hungarian. The "soldiers carrying clubs", the courtiers

"ornamented all over with diamonds", the royal children "ornamented with hearts" and the gardeners with their spades are all of course references to the four suits of cards. No such homonymy exists in Hungarian between the words corresponding to the two meanings of "clubs", "diamonds", "hearts", and "spades". In Kosztolányi's text no effort seems to have been made to translate the plural meanings, or even to choose one and leave out the rest: there is no mention of clubs, diamonds or spades in either sense.[2]

One of the biggest difficulties in translating this section is finding an equivalent for "Queen of Hearts". The card is called *kőr dáma* in Hungarian, *kőr* being the transliteration of the French word *cœur* 'heart', and *dáma* the Hungarian word for 'dame'. The term *kőr* is only used in the context of cards, the standard word for 'heart' being *szív*. Keeping the name of the card would then mean losing the reference to royalty (a dame is not a queen) as well as the irony of the epithet (Carroll's Queen of Hearts is a horrible person intensely disliked by all other characters). Where Kosztolányi has *Szív Királynő* 'Queen of Hearts' and the Varró siblings have *Kőr Dáma* 'Dame of Cœurs', I chose the hybrid *Kőr Királynő* 'Queen of Cœurs', as I felt that it was important to emphasize the contrast between the power this characters wields, which enables her to repeatedly pronounce the order "Off with his head!", and the fact that ultimately she is only a piece of cardboard.

2 This is one of the instances where Kosztolányi's 1935 *Évike* and Szobotka's 1974 version differ considerably. Kosztolányi gets rid of the Queen altogether and her role is taken on by the King; he manages to incorporate card-related puns into the Hungarian, but these are Hungarian playing cards with different suits and corresponding symbols. Szobotka turns this into a more faithful but less entertaining text by sticking to the wording of the English but omitting the card references altogether.

The name of the Cheshire-Cat represents a similar challenge for the Hungarian translator. Kosztolányi has *Fakutya* 'Wooden Dog', a reference to the peculiar saying "grins like the wooden dog". Zsuzsa and Dániel Varró opted for *Nevető Macska* 'Laughing Cat'. I wanted something that sounded like an existing expression, corresponded to the illustrations, and also retained the element of grinning. *Famacska* 'Wooden Cat' is similar to *Fakutya*, and, in case the reference is not straightforward enough, the Duchess reinforces the connection in Chapter VI:

> „Nem tudtam, hogy a famacskák mindig vigyorognak. Ami azt illeti, azt sem tudtam, hogy a macskák *tudnak* vigyorogni."
>
> „Mind tudnak, fakutyák is, famacskák is"—így a Hercegnő, „és legtöbbjük vigyorog is."
>
> ["I didn't know that wooden cats always grinned; in fact, I didn't know that cats *could* grin."
>
> "They all can, wooden dogs and wooden cats," said the Duchess; "and most of 'em do."]

A detailed analysis of all existing translations of *Alice* is beyond the scope of this foreword, but I must briefly mention the 2009 translation by the Varró siblings, which rectified many of the problems, or what seem like problems from a twenty-first-century perspective, in Kosztolányi's version. Zsuzsa Varró's prose is a relatively accurate representation, rather than a creative rewriting, of Carroll's *Alice*, although some of her decisions might seem unjustified (for example, *Dina* becomes *Durci* 'Sulky', the Dormouse is turned into a Wombat, and "Duchess" is rendered as *Baronesz* 'Baroness', an unrecognizable word for most readers, and certainly for most children). However, as far as the poems are concerned, Dániel Varró has very much imposed his own poetic style on

the Hungarian text. Similarly to his own poetry, he coins new compounds such as *hal-igától* 'from the fish-yoke' to create amusing and clever rhymes (*aligátor—hal-igától*), he uses eye-dialect to mimic contemporary casual speech (*lécci* 'pleez'), and he expands the simple four-line poem read by the White Rabbit at the trial into a feat of wit full of internal rhymes and assonance:

„Jól eloroztam a legszebb kekszet,
Most ti nem esztek kekszet, nesztek!"

[I cleverly stole the prettiest biscuit,
so there, now you won't eat biscuit].

The end result is a Hungarian translation that is a joy to read, but one that gives little idea of Carroll's style to the Hungarian reader who is unable to read the original.

My aim has been to prepare a translation that is accurate enough for a bilingual edition, but is enjoyable and flows smoothly. I tried to transpose the humour in the English text to the Hungarian as far as possible while remaining true to the spirit of the original; whether or not I have succeeded is for the reader to decide. I translated most of the poetry fairly literally, with the exception of "*Twinkle, twinkle little bat*", which is well known to the contemporary English audience: here I rewrote a similarly popular Hungarian song. In "The Mock-Turtle's Story" I used a slightly modified version of Mihály Babits's translation of Dante ("*A Szeretet mozgat napot és minden csillagot*"), and János Arany's translation of Shakespeare ("*Légy, minő vagy, kedvesem*").

I am grateful to Michael Everson for his expert advice and his willingness to publish the work of an emerging translator. I am also indebted to my friend and colleague Anna Kőszeghy for her constructive suggestions regarding the Hungarian text. This translation is dedicated to my wonder-

ful grandmother, Judit, herself a translator, who taught me the basics many years ago.

Anikó Szilágyi
Glasgow 2013

Bibliography

Józan, Ildikó. [n.d.]. "Nyelvek poétikája: Alice, Évike, Kosztolányi meg a szakirodalom és a fordítás" [Poetics of Languages: Alice, Évike, Kosztolányi, Criticism and Translation]. *Filológiai Közlöny* 2010 (3): 213–238.

Carroll, Lewis. 1935. *Évike Tündérországban* [Evie in Fairyland]. Translated by Dezső Kosztolányi. Budapest: Gergely R.

Carroll, Lewis. 1974. *Alice Csodaországban* [Alice's Adventures in Wonderland]. Edited by Tibor Szobotka. Translated by Dezső Kosztolányi. Budapest: Móra. mek.oszk.hu/00300/00348/html/.

Carroll, Lewis. 2000. "Alice's Adventures in Wonderland". In *The Annotated Alice: The Definitive Edition*, ed. Martin Gardner, 11–127. New York and London: W. W. Norton & Company.

Carroll, Lewis. 2009. *Aliz kalandjai Csodaországban és a tükör másik oldalán* [Alice's Adventures in Wonderland and on the Other Side of the Mirror]. Translated by Zsuzsa Varró and Dániel Varró. Budapest: Sziget Könyvkiadó.

A rovásírás tipográfiájáról

A rovásírás egy rúnajellegű írás a magyar nyelv lejegyzésére; a *rovásírás* név rövidített formája, a *rovás* is használatos. Az akadémiai konszenzus szerint a rovásírás végső soron az ótürk írással közös őstől eredeztethető (lásd Róna-Tas 1987, 1988),[1] feltehetőleg a 9. században került a magyarok által a Kárpát-medencébe, és figyelembe véve az ótürkkel való kapcsolatát, az i. sz. 5-8. század körül kellett kialakulnia. Első feljegyzésünk róla a késő 13. századból való, az első fennmaradt jelsor körülbelül 1490 és 1526 közé tehető (Szelp 2011).[2] A történelmi korpusz viszonylag kicsi, kezdve a rövid kőfeliratoktól, a korai

1 Róna-Tas András. 1987. *On the Development and Origin of the East Turkic "Runic" Script*. Acta Orientalia Academiae Scientiarum Hung. Tomus XLI (1), 7-14 (1987); Róna-Tas András. 1988. "Problems of the East European scripts with special regard to the newly found inscriptions of Szarvas", in *Settimane di studio del Centro italiano di studi sull'alto medioevo 35. Popoli delle steppe: Unni, Avari, Ungari,* Spoleto, 23-29 aprile 1987 (published 1988), Spoleto, 483–511.

2 Szelp Szabolcs. 2011. "A Nikolsburgi ábécé szerzősége és keletkezési ideje", in *Magyar Nyelv* 107, Budapest, 407–428.
Also online: http://www.c3.hu/~magyarnyelv/11-4/szelp_114.pdf

tudományos munkákon át a késő humanista időszakból, egészen a díszítő vagy titkosírásszerű alkalmazásig.

A 20. század során több kísérlet is történt a történelmi ábécé kibővítésére annak érdekében, hogy az jobban igazodjon a modern magyar íráshoz. A rovásírás manapság számottevő használói körrel rendelkezik. Például a férj és feleség Szakács Gábor és Friedrich Klára beutazzák a történelmi Magyarország területeit, és nyári ill. téli tanfolyamokon valamint egyéb kulturális rendezvényeken tanítják a rovásírást és rovásírás tanárokat. Nemzetközi versenyeket rendeznek majd egy évtizede, több tízezer gyermek részvételével, többek között fogalmazás rovásírásban való lejegyzése és a kalligráfia terén megméretve.

A rovásábécé érdekes, de ugyanakkor kihívást is jelent a tipográfus számára. A legtöbb jelenleg használatos betűtípus optikailag azonos vonalvastagságú talpatlan (sans-serif) betűtípus, és ezekből is viszonylag kicsi a választék. Ennek a sajátos stílusú sorozat részeként megjelenő, 27.000 szóból álló regénynek a rovásírásos kiadásával kapcsolatban ugyazokat a kérdéseket kellett feltennem magamnak, mint amik az *Aliz* niktográf szögletes, Ewell-i, Shaw-i és unifon kiadásai kapcsán felmerültek. Ezekhez hasonló stílusban terveztem meg a rovásírás betűrajzolatait is: „Csodaországban" 'Wonderland' De Vinne roman betűtípusban 𐲆𐲛𐲇𐲀𐲛𐲢𐲥𐲁𐲍𐲂𐲀𐲙; *De Vinne italic* betűtípusban *𐲆𐲛𐲇𐲀𐲛𐲢𐲥𐲁𐲍𐲂𐲀𐲙*; Mona Lisa Recut betűtípusban 𐲆𐲛𐲇𐲀𐲛𐲢𐲥𐲁𐲍𐲂𐲀𐲙; ENGRAVERS ROMAN betűtípusban 𐲆𐲛𐲇𐲀𐲛𐲢𐲥𐲁𐲍𐲂𐲀𐲙; **ENGRAVERS ROMAN BOLD** betűtípusban pedig **𐲆𐲛𐲇𐲀𐲛𐲢𐲥𐲁𐲍𐲂𐲀𐲙**.

A kis- és nagybetűk rendszere a rovásírásban a XX. században fejlődött ki, bár Szamosközi István egy 1604-es kéziratában is feltűnik már. Formájukat tekintve a kisbetűk egyszerűen a nagybetűk kisebb változatai. Bár a *Rudimentá*ban a 𐲦 *T* betűnek van egy kis lenyúló szára a latin „y", betűével hasonló szögben húzva, modern anyagokban nem

találkoztam fel- és lenyúló szárakkal történő kísérletezéssel, úgyhogy én is ragaszkodtam a hagyományhoz.

Bár az itt használt betűtípusok a rovásírásos művek többségénél valamivel bonyolultabbak, remélem, hogy az *Aliz kalandjai Csodaországban* jelen kiadása könnyen megszokható és kellemes olvasmány lesz.

𐲀𐳖𐳐𐳯 𐳓𐳀𐳖𐳀𐳙𐳇𐳒𐳀𐳐 𐲆𐳛𐳇𐳀𐳛𐳢𐳥𐳁𐳍𐳂𐳀𐳙

𐲀𐳖𐳐𐳯 𐳓𐳀𐳖𐳀𐳙𐳇𐳒𐳀𐳐 𐲆𐳛𐳇𐳀𐳛𐳢𐳥𐳁𐳍𐳂𐳀𐳙

𐲀𐳖𐳐𐳯 𐳓𐳀𐳖𐳀𐳙𐳇𐳒𐳀𐳐 𐲆𐳛𐳇𐳀𐳛𐳢𐳥𐳁𐳍𐳂𐳀𐳙

𐲀𐳖𐳐𐳯 𐳓𐳀𐳖𐳀𐳙𐳇𐳒𐳀𐳐 𐲆𐳛𐳇𐳀𐳛𐳢𐳥𐳁𐳍𐳂𐳀𐳙

𐲀𐳖𐳐𐳯 𐳓𐳀𐳖𐳀𐳙𐳇𐳒𐳀𐳐 𐲆𐳛𐳇𐳀𐳛𐳢𐳥𐳁𐳍𐳂𐳀𐳙

Michael Everson
Portlaoise 2016

A rovásábécé

A lenti táblázat a rovásábécé betűit sorolja fel. A nagybetűk után a kisbetűk következnek, utánuk pedig a betűk modern magyar megfelelői. Érdemes megjegyezni, hogy a magyar kettőzött mássalhangzót jelölő hármas betűket, például *ggy*, *lly*, *nny*, *ssz* és *tty*, a rovásírásban kettős betűkkel jelölik: 𐳎𐳎 *gygy*, 𐳗𐳗 *lyly*, 𐳚𐳚 *nyny*, 𐳥𐳥 *szsz*, és 𐳨𐳨 *tyty*.

𐲍	𐲌	𐲋	𐲉	𐲇	𐲆	𐲄	𐲂	𐲁	𐲀
𐳍	𐳌	𐳋	𐳉	𐳇	𐳆	𐳄	𐳂	𐳁	𐳀
g	f	é	e	d	cs	c	b	á	a
𐲙	𐲘	𐲗	𐲖	𐲓	𐲒	𐲑	𐲐	𐲏	𐲎
𐳙	𐳘	𐳗	𐳖	𐳓	𐳒	𐳑	𐳐	𐳏	𐳎
n	m	ly	l	k	j	í	i	h	gy
𐲦	𐲥	𐲤	𐲢	𐲠	𐲟	𐲞	𐲜	𐲛	𐲚
𐳦	𐳥	𐳤	𐳢	𐳠	𐳟	𐳞	𐳜	𐳛	𐳚
t	sz	s	r	p	ő	ö	ó	o	ny
		𐲰	𐲯	𐲮	𐲬	𐲭	𐲫	𐲪	𐲨
		𐳰	𐳯	𐳮	𐳬	𐳭	𐳫	𐳪	𐳨
		zs	z	v	ű	ü	ú	u	ty

On Old Hungarian Typography

The Old Hungarian script is a runiform script used to write the Hungarian language. In Hungarian it is called *rovásírás* 'incised script', from rovás 'incision' and *írás* 'writing, script'; sometimes *rovásírás* is abbreviated to *rovás* alone. The academic consensus is that Old Hungarian ultimately derives from a common ancestor with the Old Turkic script,[1] and appears to have been brought by the Magyars to the Carpathian Basin in the 9th century CE, and, owing to its link with the Old Turkic script, it must have been developed around the 5th–8th century CE. Old Hungarian is first mentioned in a written account of the late 13th century; the first surviving alphabetical listing dates to between 1490

1 Róna-Tas András. 1987. *On the Development and Origin of the East Turkic "Runic" Script.* Acta Orientalia Academiae Scientiarum Hung. Tomus XLI (1), 7-14 (1987); Róna-Tas András. 1988. "Problems of the East European scripts with special regard to the newly found inscriptions of Szarvas", in *Settimane di studio del Centro italiano di studi sull'alto medioevo 35. Popoli delle steppe: Unni, Avari, Ungari,* Spoleto, 23-29 aprile 1987 (published 1988), Spoleto, 483–511.

and 1526.[2] The historical corpus is relatively small, beginning with the short stone-carved inscriptions, and leading to a corpus of early scholarly work from the late humanist period, and subsequently to a body of material where the script was used as a decorative or as a secret cipher script.

In the twentieth century several attempts have been undertaken to extend the historic alphabet so that it corresponds better to modern Hungarian orthography. Old Hungarian enjoys a fair amount of current use. The husband-and-wife team Gábor Szakács and Klára Friedrich, for example, are activists who travel throughout the former lands of the Kingdom of Hungary, teaching Old Hungarian and training teachers at summer-schools, winter-schools, and other cultural events. International competitions have been held for nearly a decade, with tens of thousands of children participating in a variety of activities, including creative writing in Old Hungarian and calligraphy.

The Old Hungarian alphabet is both interesting to and problematic for the typographer. Most current fonts are monoline sans-serif fonts and not a great deal of choice is available. In the context of publishing a 27,000-word novel in a series of books with a particular house style, I had to ask myself the same questions for Old Hungarian that I did for my editions of *Alice* in the Nyctographic Square Alphabet, in the Ewellic Alphabet, in the Shavian Alphabet, and in the Unifon Alphabet. Here, as for those books, I chose to design letterforms for Old Hungarian in the same style; "Csodaországban" 'Wonderland' in De Vinne roman is ↄ1Xʌ4IHↄ1+ↄꝊ and in *De Vinne italic* is *ↄ1Xʌ4IHↄ1+ↄꝊ*; in Mona Lisa Recut it is ↄ1Xʌ4IHↄ1+ↄꝊ, in Engravers Roman it is ↄ1Xʌ4IHↄ1+ↄꝊ, and in **Engravers Roman Bold** it is **ↄ1Xʌ4IHↄ1+ↄꝊ**.

2 Szelp Szabolcs. 2011. "A Nikolsburgi ábécé szerzősége és keletkezési ideje", in *Magyar Nyelv* 107, Budapest, 407–428.
Also online: http://www.c3.hu/~magyarnyelv/11-4/szelp_114.pdf

Casing in Old Hungarian was developed in the twentieth century, though it appears in a 1604 manuscript by István Szamosközi. The shapes of the lower-case letters are simply smaller versions of the upper-case letters. Although in the *Rudimenta* the letter [illegible] *T* has a bit of a descender, drawn at an angle like the Latin letter "y", I have never seen experiments with ascenders or descenders in revivalist materials, so I remained conservative here.

Although the fonts used in this edition are somewhat more elaborate than those found in many works in the Old Hungarian alphabet, I hope that readers will find this edition of *Alice's Adventures in Wonderland* pleasant to read, with only a short period of accustomization.

[illegible]

[illegible]

[illegible]

[illegible]

[illegible]

Michael Everson

Portlaoise 2016

The Old Hungarian Alphabet

The chart below lists the Old Hungarian letters. First the capital letters are given, then the small letters, then the representation of the letters in standard Hungarian orthography. Note that some trigraphs in Hungarian which represent geminate consonants, like *ggy*, *lly*, *nny*, *ssz*, and *tty* are represented by digraphs in Old Hungarian: 𐳎𐳎 *gygy*, 𐳗𐳗 *lyly*, 𐳚𐳚 *nyny*, 𐳥𐳥 *szsz*, and 𐳨𐳨 *tyty*.

𐲍	𐲌	𐲋	𐲉	𐲇	𐲆	𐲄	𐲂	𐲁	𐲀
𐳍	𐳌	𐳋	𐳉	𐳇	𐳆	𐳄	𐳂	𐳁	𐳀
g	f	é	e	d	cs	c	b	á	a
𐲙	𐲘	𐲗	𐲖	𐲓	𐲒	𐲑	𐲐	𐲏	𐲎
𐳙	𐳘	𐳗	𐳖	𐳓	𐳒	𐳑	𐳐	𐳏	𐳎
n	m	ly	l	k	j	í	i	h	gy
𐲦	𐲥	𐲤	𐲢	𐲠	𐲟	𐲝	𐲜	𐲛	𐲚
𐳦	𐳥	𐳤	𐳢	𐳠	𐳟	𐳝	𐳜	𐳛	𐳚
t	sz	s	r	p	ő	ö	ó	o	ny
		𐲰	𐲯	𐲮	𐲭	𐲬	𐲫	𐲪	𐲨
		𐳰	𐳯	𐳮	𐳭	𐳬	𐳫	𐳪	𐳨
		zs	z	v	ű	ü	ú	u	ty

PAŦH ◊PΛPCŦꟼPŦ

ЏCŦPCHIPΛXPC

[illegible]

I. [illegible] 7

II. [illegible] 15

III. [illegible] 23

IIII. [illegible] 30

V. [illegible] 39

VI. [illegible] 50

VII. [illegible] 61

VIII. [illegible] 70

VIIII. [illegible] 80

X. [illegible] 89

XI. [illegible]? 98

XII. [illegible] 106

ВᆢОСН ЕЄ†тА О†ᑭЕᑭ† ᑭ
◊СЕЕЕАЄᑭЄВ ОМᑭᑭ,
Λ ОКDКНАКО, ХС‡ АЄАОКИЕАЄХХ
⊗СОᑭᑭС†ᑭСС МᑭᑭР,
◊СНМАХᑭС ᑭХС Нᑭ ᑭ МᑭАᑭІ,
ХС‡ ВСΛᑭ ОЄЕ†ᑭЄВ МІНᑭ.

ᒐООСЕЕ ‡ЕΩΛᑭ ΛСО ⊗МНΩᑭ ОᑭАᑭС†
ᒐ‡НЄ Сᑭ‡СХХ ІᑭВХᑭС,
СЄᑭᑭКС-СЄᑭᑭ Т‡ ΩС†ᑭСНІᑭА,
ХᑭАААᑭᑭᑭᑭО ЄО ХᑭНВᑭС,
Λ ᑭАОСDᑭᑭНᑭ ХᑭЕᑭСНᑭ ᑭ
ΩССᑭО Сᑭ‡ М††ᑭᑭВᑭС.

ᑭАтИ! ⊗СΛ† Є ‡ЄНВЄОВЄΛСᑭ,
Λ ⊗†ССВ, ‡ЄСΛС† ОСЕЕЄА
‡ЄНВЄОᑭАВСО ВЄААС ⊗ЄОᑭЄΛ†,
ВЄОЄОНЄ Хᑭ ССЕЄА,
НЄᑭᑭСОЄΛ СΛ ΩС†ᑭАᑭᑭСΛ,
ВЄІІ† ⊗КА†НЄ СНІ ЄА.

ЯCAŦ ЯЄAAƐYY, AƐMƐYY HCAY ŦƐ „CFHFCЦAƐOMFH" ⊗ЄAŦHFYM XЄ⊗ƐYYƐAЧMƐAƐY, ŦƐ AƐACŦFCXX ЦFACŦFAFHF ЧHƐA MCAY. CƐB FOFHYF ƐAŦCXCŦ, CƐЯCŦ HFƐAAƐC MFAFOŦHƐ CŦFAƐCY CA ЯƐAKAƐƐ, MŦЯCŦ ЯЦЯFCFA OЖHXƐC XƐYƐYYƐ FƐ ƐŦŦO ƐƐOHƆXƐ.

„XFY" — AƆCŦCAYF PAŦЯ ЯFAFXFƆ, „ƐŦ ŦO⊗C ƐACA MYFC F AƐƐƐƐC AƐAMHMACŦ ŦAFЯFC AƐЯЯŦACA AƐƐ! ЯŦ⊗C XFYCHCFO ⊗CACFO YFHYFCŦ CYYЯƐC! ЯƐA AƐ ⊗CACO ЯMOOFCCŦ, ЯCA FOOCH AƐ, XF AƐƐAƐЯ F XЯЯYƐYƐHƐA!" (ƐXXƐC MFACƐŦCЦAƐA ŦAFЯF ŦA MCAY.)

ƐŦHƐ ЦFO ЯMЯFCY, ЯMЯFCY AƐ⊗ƐAƐ. MFFCC ACAƐ CH AƐ FƐ FAFFHF? „OTMFCЦŦ MFŦCO, XFD OŦACЯƐYƐHY ЯMЯFCYFЯ ƐŦŦŦA" — ЯCCŦYF ⊗ƐCCЯFCACC. „XŦЯFCA OЖЯƐAƐŦO F ⊗ЖAŦ OЖЯƐЯƐCCYFF ⊗ƐAƐ. AFAAMO ЦFO: FOOCH XFYƐЯƐHЖYFЯ OŦACЯƐYƐH ЯƐOƐC AƐCCƐO, FЯY XŦƐƐЯ..." (YMŦŦFYCO, PAŦЯ ACO ŦOƐAЯŦY ЯƐAYFCMAY FƐ ŦAOCAFXFC, CA XFH ƐƐ CƐЯ MCAY OŦЯCCŦCYYFC FC AƐЯЯYƐACA FHHF, XCŦ ƐAŦŦЦƐOŦŦƐC F YMŦFAFMFA, XŦƐƐC AƐCOŦ CƐЯ XFAAACYYF, ЯŦY ЯCCŦ, ŦFOCHAFACFO FC MCAY) „...ŦAƐC, OЖHЧAXƐAЧA ŦO⊗C XCƐƐM MYFY YƐЯƐYYƐЯ ЯƐA, ŦƐ MFFCC ЯŦ⊗C ƐCAƐAACAŦ CA XCƐƐMAFAŦ OЖHЖC MFŦCO?" (PAŦЯCFO ⊗CAFAЯF AƐЯ MCAY HCAF, ЯŦ FƐ F ƐCAƐAACAŦ CA XCƐƐMAFAŦ OЖH, ŦƐ MŦ ACCŦCAYF, CFŦƐƐHЦ OŦ⊗ƐƐƐЯCAƐO.)

CƐЯACOFHF MFHF OƐЯŦYƐ. „OTMFCЦŦ MFŦCO, XCŦ OƐHƐYƐЧA ⊗CACO-Ɛ ƐACŦ F ⊗ЖAŦЖC! ЯŦ⊗C MŦŦŦƐA AƐƐ ⊗ƐAXMOOFCCŦ CO⊗C CЯXƐHƐO OЖЯMƐY, FOŦO ⊗ƐƐŦƐA AƐ⊗ƐAƐ FFHCFO! PЯY XŦƐƐЯ, ƐO FƐ FCYŦЯƐOMACO..." (ЯCAY OŦ⊗ƐƐЯƐYYƐC ЖHЧAY, XCŦ CƐЯ XFAAAFF AƐCOŦ, ЯƐHY ƐƐ MFAFXCŦ ƐŦFAFYAFƐC CƐЯ YƐƐCY FC ƐCCFO) „...ŦƐ YMŦŦFYCO, ЯFŦŦ ЯƐA OƐAA OCHŦƐƐCƐЯ FƐ CHƐFA CƐMƐY. OCHƐЯ, FƐƐCƐCƐЯ, ƐƐ MƐ-ƎƐAFCŦ? MFŦ PMƐYHFAŦFF?" (CA ЯƐAЯHCXFAY ЯMOŦŦAŦЯCŦ, ЯŦOЖHXƐC XƐƐCAY — OƐЯƐЯƐAƐAƐYƐO ЦFO ƐA, ЯŦ⊗C AƐЯƐY ЯMOŦŦAŦЯCŦ, ЯŦOЖHXƐC F AƐMƐAƐXƐC ЯMЯFCYCO! ƐƐHŦCYƐYƐO CƐOYƐO ЯƐCCƐ?) „CA ЯŦ⊗C YMŦŦFYAFC OŦAAFDCFO ⊗CACFO YFHYFCŦ, XF ЯƐAOCHŦƐЯƐЯ! CƐЯ, AƐЯЯŦOƐЯƐC CƐЯ OCHŦƐƐЯƐYƐЯ ЯƐA: YFAFC OŦ AƐƐ THMF MFAFЯCA."

ƐŦHƐ ЦFO ЯMЯFCY, ЯMЯFCY AƐ⊗ƐAƐ. ЯŦMƐA ƐŦƐXƐY CƐЯ CFŦƐC YƐЯƐYYƐY, PAŦЯ XFЯFHCAFC MFHF XƐƐCAƐŦ OƐЯŦYƐY. „ŦŦCFCFO CFŦƐC ⊗CACO XFFCƐЯCŦ ЯF ƐAYƐ, FЯY XŦƐƐЯ!" (P ЯFЦOFF XŦMFYFO ŦŦCFCFO.) HƐЯCAƐЯ, CƐЯ ⊗ƐAƐYFYƐCFO ƐA FŦCŦ CƐOŦ ƐŦ YFAOF YƐƐƐY MFЦCHŦŦŦƐXƐC. ŦŦCF, ŦHFAFЯ!

*   *   *   *

*   *   *

*   *   *   *

[illegible]

* * * *

* * *

* * * *

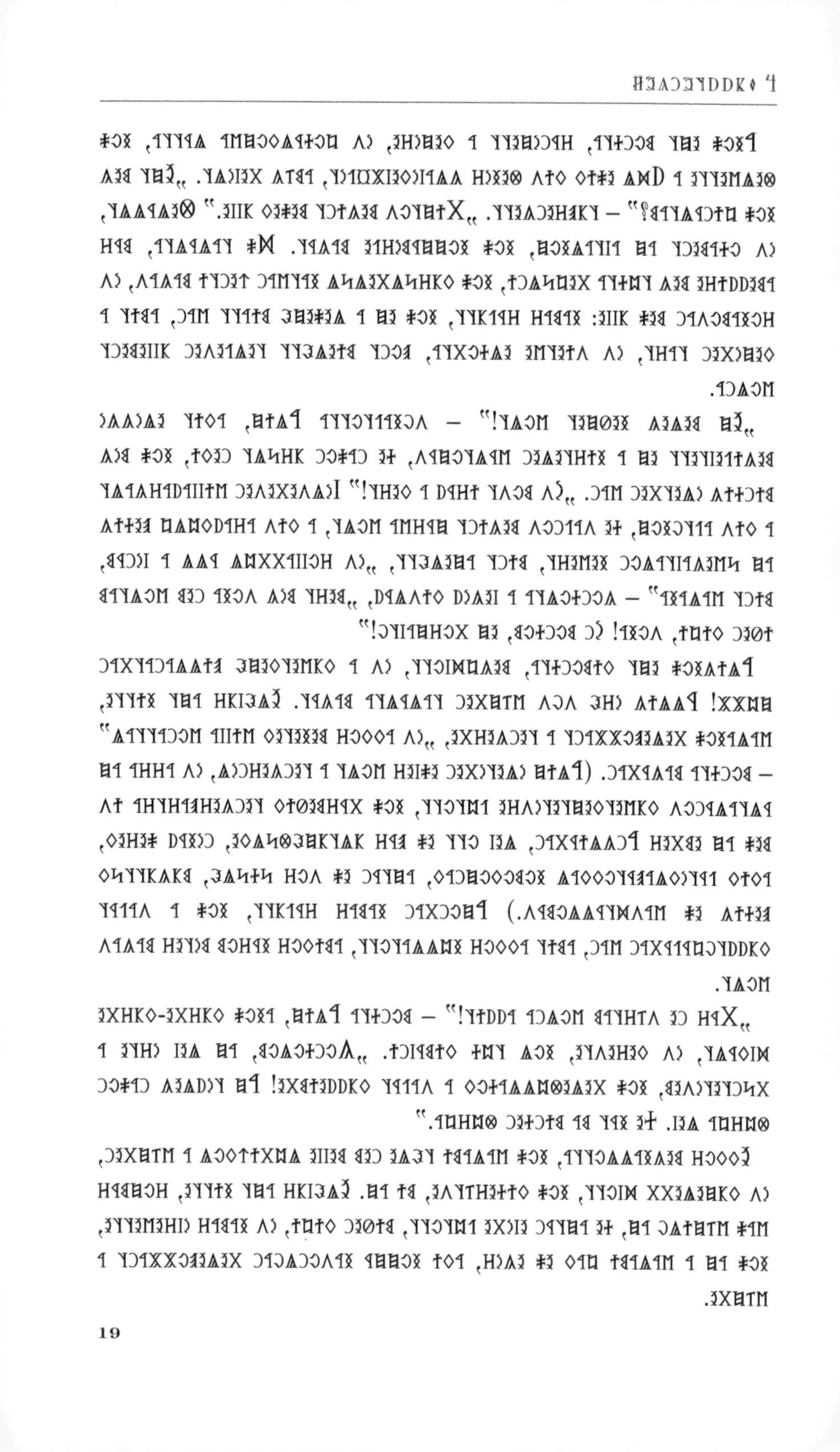

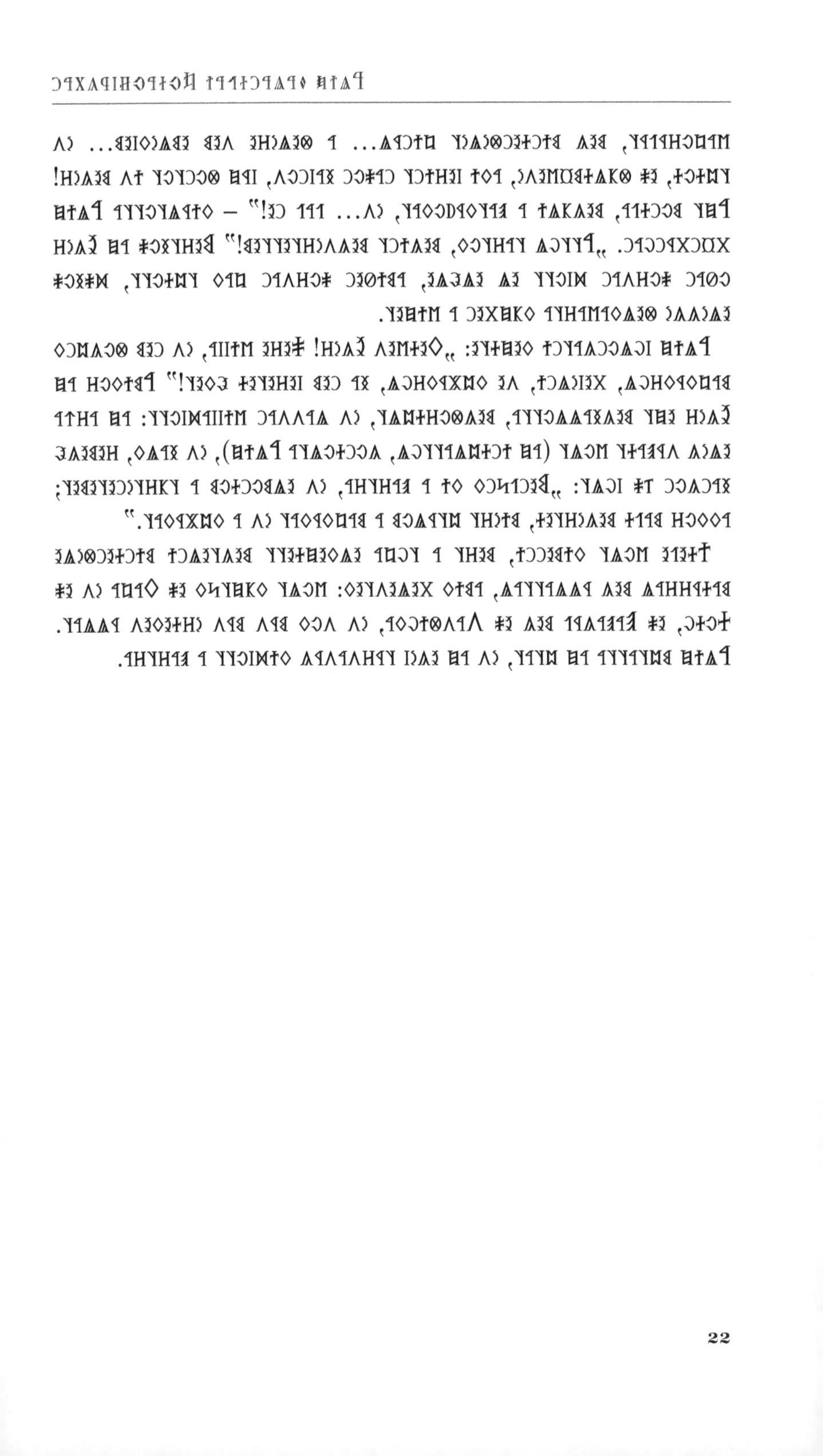

III.

„Oxkb-oxkb!" — BсСtУP PН ZАсН ⊗ссУСАОСtМP. „BtсС оСi МPtУСО? ZН P АZАiPННРХХ tсАсА, PPtУ tАВZНZО. ПZсtZУ оСНZО iСZZС BtсtZСОtУZА!

'PсААtP ССZZ, PPZОССО iНОАсАZ МсАУ МZНZУZОНZ, сА PPZО PН МУСХХt

ttZХZС СPtZС tА ZСННPiСОСУУ P оtУPОВPPОСАPАZСН сА P АZtАPНPАZСН,

ZPВPНсАPС ХZZХtсАУ ZСtУPС МtАВсАСPО, PОtСZО нtСУ P ZPPP

УPВсАPУУP. Ztwtс сА BсНоPН, BZНttP сА СНУМВХНtP МНP..."

„⊗Мi!" — BсСtУP P ZPPАPP, сА BZАНiPНОсtСУУ.

„ZPНPсПсАi?" — оСНtZНZУZ PН ZАсН ЖiiНPсtсАУ ZсВАсООРА, tZ

НсZZPсУ МtМPНttPАPС. „BссtУPА МPАPВtУ?"

„СZВ сС!" — МPАPiсАУP P ZPPАPP АtZУМZ.

„ZZttА PНУ ZtУУZВ" — BсСtУP PН ZАсН. „⊗ссУPУсВ. 'ZtМtс сА

BсНоPН, BZНttP сА СНУМВХНtP МНP, ZПАсАZУ ZАОнtЖУУ сZоt, сА BсА

ЛУtАPсt, P ZPНPОtPА ОPсУZНХМНt сНАZО tА УPсPПсАсPО АPУУP

PНУ..."

„BtУ АPУсУУ?" — оСНtZНZУZ P ОPНP.

„PНУ АPУУP" — ⊗ZАZАУZ PН ZАсН BZААZZZZУZАZС ХсiiМАPС. „BZНiZ

сtАМPС УМtсt, BtУ PZАZсУ PН, ZсZ 'PНУ'."

„СС BссУсАPС УМtсВ, BtУ PZАZсУ PН 'PНУ', ⊗ZАZА, ZP СС АPУсВ BZА" —

tZ P ОPНP, „PАУPАPХPС ХсоPУ МPZ оМоPPtсУ. P оСНtсА PН, ZсZ BtУ

АPУсУУ PН сНАZО?"

PН ZАсН СZВ МZУУ УМtсВPАУ P оСНtсАНZА, tсоPХХ ZсНАPС ⊗ссУPУУP:

„'...УPсPПсАсPО АPУУP PНУ, ZсZ ZАВZсZZС ZtАtН PУZАtсААZА

МtАВсАZсН, сА ⊗ZАPPсАPP сZоt P оСНсСУ. МtАВсА ZАZtсУZ iZНсiZС

МtАZАоZtZZУ, PВ P ссНВPсС оPУссPО iZВУZАZсАсАZ...' Zс ZАВ PААi,

оZtМZАZВ?" — ⊗сНtМАУ PАtНZсН.

„СZtМZАZС, BtсУ ZtttА" — BсСtУP PАtН ХсНМАPС. „СZВ Мt УiСсtО,

BtсУZP ZУУZА iPНttссО."

„ZН ZАZУХZС" — BсСtУP P tсtс нсСZZZсZАZС, PZсZ ⊗ZАZВZАоZtZZУ,

„iPМАА сВ PН нАсА ZАссPсАPАPУ, BtМZА ZPУPАсАPХХ BсtiZНZО

PНсссZАt ХZМZУсАсНZ..."

„ХZiсАi сНУZАВZАZС!" — iсАPАУ BZА P ЛPАОtсоP. „ZZНОсZО P ZсiiМ

iPМPОсZО P ⊗ZАсУ АZ сНУZВ, АZУ, iZНtсУZВ УZ АZВ!" PНВPА АZZZPPсУУP P

⊗ZсУ, ZсZ ZАНZiУАZ P BсАсоPУ; ссZВП BPtPН ZPААZZPPсPС ⊗ZАМtZZсАсУ.

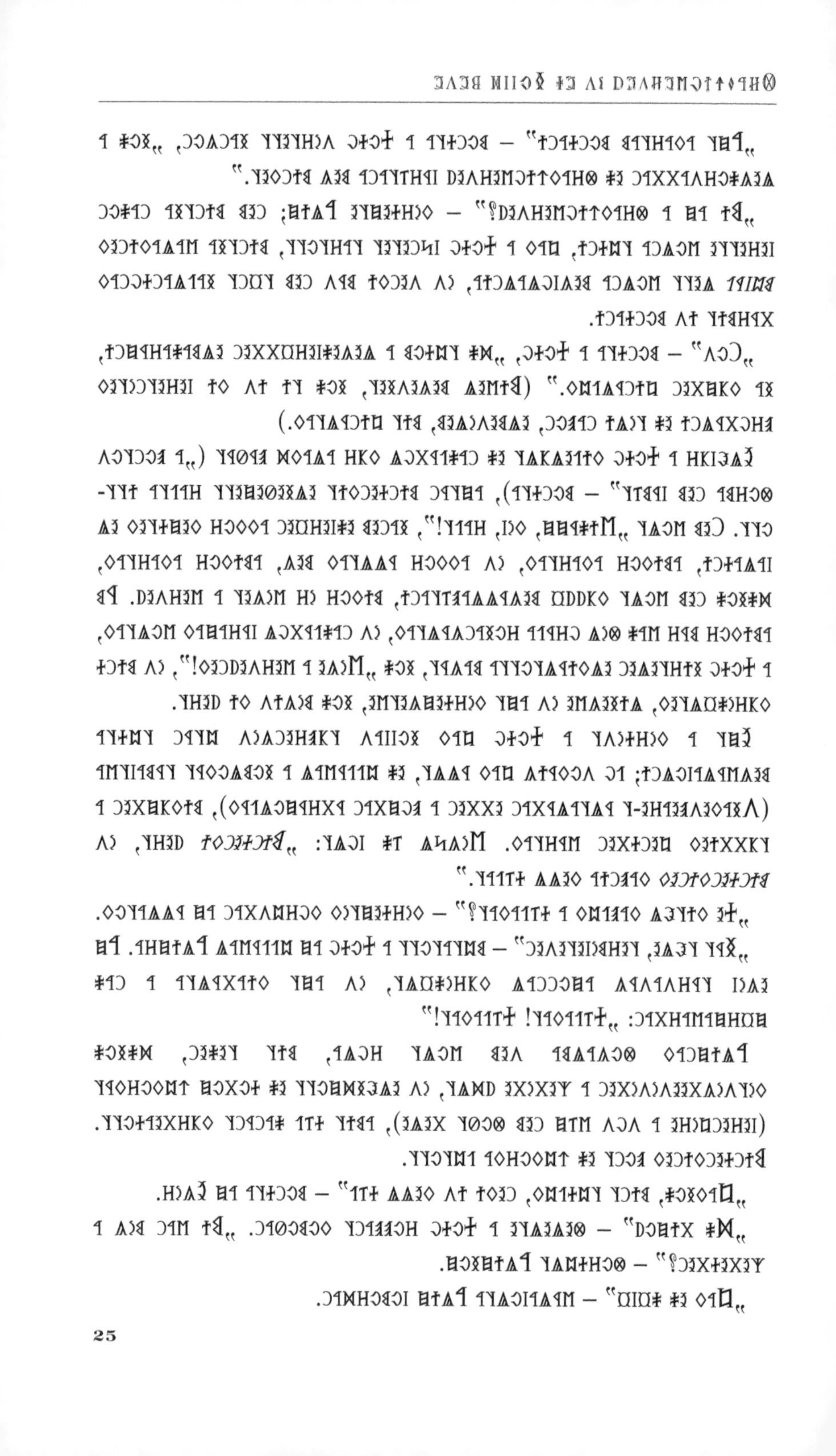

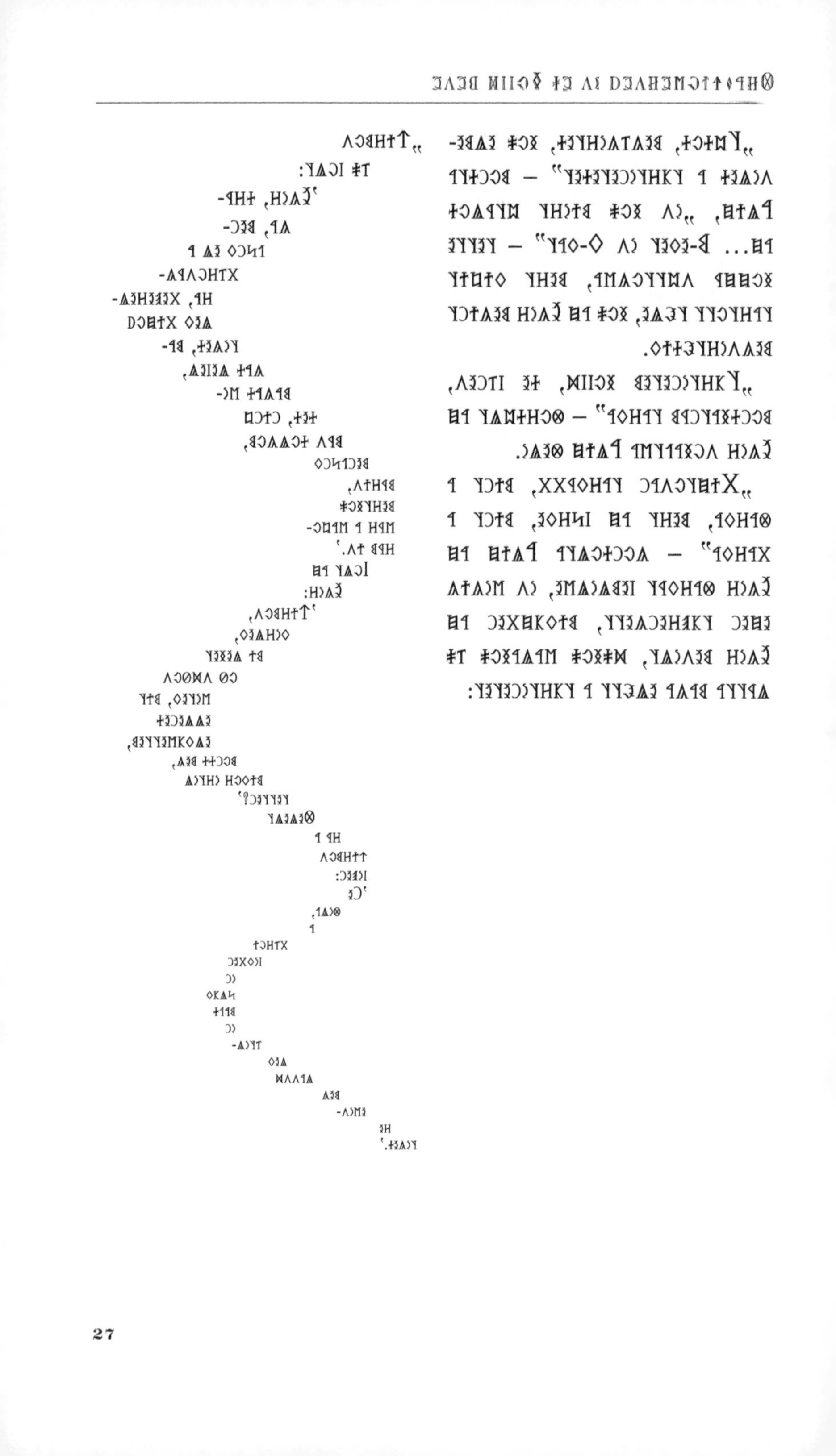

[illegible]

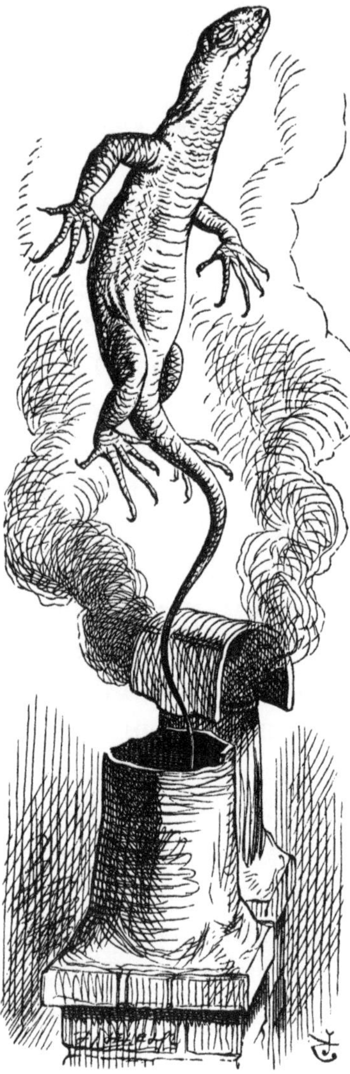

V. [illegible]

[illegible]

[illegible]

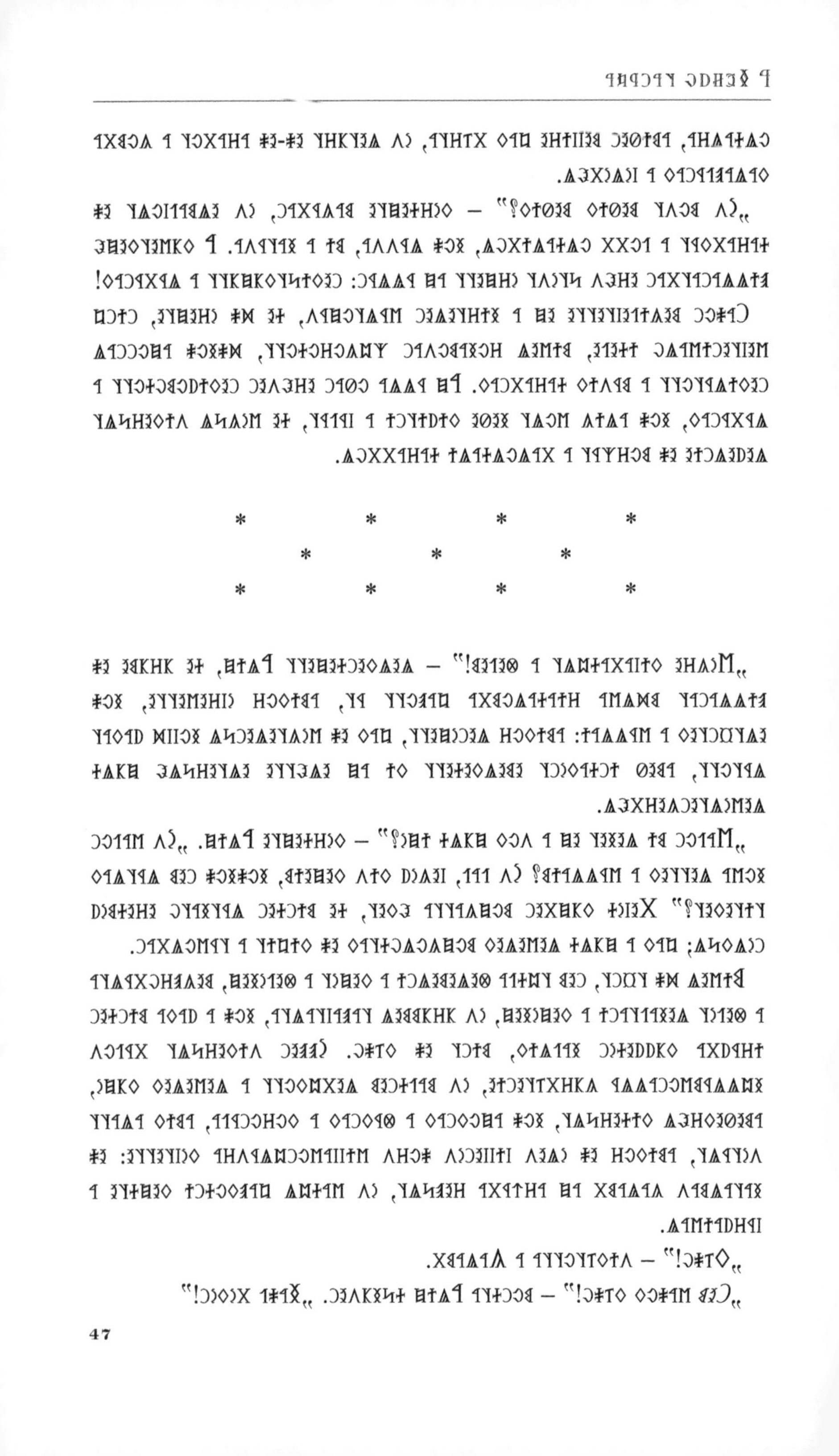

[illegible]

[illegible]

[illegible]

[illegible]

[illegible]

[illegible]

[illegible]

[illegible]

[illegible]

[illegible]

[illegible]

[illegible]

[illegible]

[illegible]

[illegible]

VI.

ꟼᴀꝉᴇ ꞔᴇꝺс ꟼꝺꝺꝉнꟼ ссмꞔꞔꞔꞔ, ꭓсǂ мꝉııꟼ оꞔᴀᴀꞔꞔ ıꟼᴀꟼꝉсꝉꟼ ꟼᴇ ꞔнꝉꞔꭓꞔ, сꭓꭓсǂ ʙꞔᴀꭓꟼᴀᴀꟼꟼо, ꟼʙꝉосн ꞔꞔꝉꝉᴀ ᴀꞔᴀокᴇꞔᴀꞔꭓꭓ оꝉомомпоꟼᴀꞔ, ꟼ ꭓꟼᴀ-ꝉсꟼᴧ ʙꟼн ꞔᴀʙꞔсꞔ, ꟼ Хсоꟼ-ꝉсꟼᴧ ꞔꞔꝉꝉᴀ ꟼᴇ ꟼꟼꞔс окᴇꞔᴀсꭓꞔс чᴀꞔ ꟼ ⊗ᴀкꝉꞔс, сᴧ хмꞔꟼс хꟼʙмᴀꞔꟼ ꟼᴇ ꞔᴀꞔꞔ.

ꟼᴀꝉᴇ ⊗ᴀссосс ꟼᴇ ꟼꟼꞔсꭓᴇ сᴧссꞔ, сᴧ хꞔосꞔсᴀсꞔꞔ.

„Сꝉсп снꞔꞔᴀʙꞔ осꞔсᴀсꝉ" — ıсᴀꟼᴀꞔ ʙꞔᴀ ꟼᴇ ꝉсꟼᴧ, „ʙꞔᴀꞔꞔꝉꝉᴀ оꞔꞔ сохсᴀ. ꞔᴀꞔıкн ꝉᴧ, ʙꞔнꞔ ꟼᴇ ꟼꟼꞔссꟼо мǂꟼсꟼᴇсс ꟼᴇ сᴀꝉꟼᴀꟼс мꟼǂсо, ʙꝉсꞔ ꞔꞔ; ʙꟼᴧсꝉıсн ꝉᴧ, ʙꞔнꞔ сøꟼс сꟼǂ ꟼ ᴇꟼꟼ сꝉꟼꭓꞔсꞔ, ꭓсǂ оꝉᴇꟼнꞔ, ꭓсǂ хꟼноꝉ ꝉᴧ ʙꞔᴀꭓꟼᴀᴀꟼꟼ." Сᴧ мꟼᴀсхꟼс, нсꞔꞔꟼсꞔ очᴀкск ᴧ ᴇꟼꟼ ꭓꟼᴀᴀꟼꟼıсꞔꞔ хꞔсꞔнꞔᴀ: ⊗сøꟼʙꟼꞔсᴧ хкʙхкᴀсᴧ ʙꞔᴀ ꞔчııкᴀсᴧ, сᴧ ꝉꝉꞔсоссꞔ ꞔǂ сꟼǂ нсхꟼꟼ, ʙꝉсꞔꭓꟼ ꞔǂ ꞔꟼᴀ мꟼǂ оꟼссꟼ ꝉꟼнхсонꟼ ꞔкнꞔ мсᴀсꟼ.

„Осн꞉ʙ" — ʙссꝉꞔꟼ ꟼᴀꝉᴇ, „ꟼоосн ꭓсǂ ıмꞔсо хꞔ?"

Нꙮꙋɔɔ

(ꟼꙋɔΛ ꟼ ІꟼОꟼꙋɔƐ ɔΛ ꟼ ХꟼХꟼ ꟸΛ ХꙋОꟼꟼꙋɔΛɔꟸɔꟼꟼ):

„Ɔꟼ! ɔꟼ! ɔꟼ!"

ꙞꟸОꙋХꙋɔ ꟼ ꙞꙋНꟸꙋΛɔƐ ꟼ ꙞꟼΛɔꟸꟸО ꙋꙋНІІꟼОɔꟼ ɔɔꙋОꙋΛꟼꙋ, ꟸꙋНꙋꟼɔ ꙮꙋΛ-ꙮΛꙋꟸɔХꟼꟼ ꟼ ХꟼХꟼꟼ, ꟼОꟸ, ꙋΛꙋԀ, ꙋꟸ ꙋɔԀꟸꟼɔꟼꟼ, ꙋɔꟸ ꟼΛꟸꙋ ꟼΛꟸΛ ꙋꟼΛΛɔꟼꟼꟼ ꟼ ІꙋꙋꙋΛꙋꟼ:

„ꟼꙋɔНꟼ ɔНꟸꙋꙋΛ ꟼ ꟸꙋНꙋꙋО
ꟸОꙋɔ ꟸꙋНꙋꟼ ΛɔНΛɔꟼ,
ꙞɔНꟼ ꙋꟼ ɔꙋꙋ ꙋꟸ ꟼꟼНꟼꟼꟼ Оꙋꟸꙋꙋ,
Хꟸꙋꙋꟼ ꙋ ꟼ ХɔНΛɔꟼ!"

Нꙮꙋɔɔ

„Ɔꟼ! ɔꟼ! ɔꟼ!"

„ꟼꙋΛΛɔО! ꟸꟼꟼОꟼΛꙋꟼꟼɔꟸ ꙋꟸ Оꟸꙋꟸꟼ, ꙋꟼ ꟼОꟼНɔꟸ!" – Ꙟɔɔꟸꟼꟼ ꟼ ꙞꙋНꟸꙋΛɔƐ ꟼΛꟸꙋɔꟼО, ꟼꙋɔꟸ ɔꟸꙋꙋꟼꟸꟸɔꟼꟼ ɔꙋОꟸ ꟼ ХꟼХꟼꟼ. „ꙞꙋɔɔꙞ ОꙋΛΛ ОɔꟼꟼΛꙋꟸɔꟸ ꟼ ОꟸНꟼОɔꙋꟸ ОНɔОꙋꟼꟼ-ꟼꟼꟼІꙞꟼНꟼ" – ꟼꙋꙋꟼΛ ОꟸΛꟸꙋꟼꙋꟼꟼ ꟼ ІɔХꟼХɔΛ. ꟼ ІꟼОꟼꙋɔƐ ꙋꟼꟼɔꟼꙋꟼꟸꟸꟼɔꟼꟼ ꙋꟸ ΛꙋНꙋꙋԀꙋꟼ, ꟸꙋ Ꙟɔɔꟼꟼ ꙋΛꙋꙋꙋꙋꟼꙋ.

ꟼΛꟸꙋɔꟼО ОꟸΛΛɔ ɔɔꙋꙋꙋɔ ΛꟸОꙋНꙋΛꟼ ꙋΛОꟼꙋɔꟸꟼ ꟼ ХꟼХꟼꟼ, ꙞꟸꙋꙋΛ ꙮꙋНꙋꟼ ꙮɔНꙞꟼꟼꙋ ꙋꙋꙋΛΛɔΛ ꙋɔΛꟼ; ꙞꟸɔꟸɔꙮꙋΛɔ ꙞꙋНꟸꙋꙋꟼꟼО ꟼ ОꟼНꟼꟸꟸ ꙞꙋΛ ꟼ ΛꟼХꟼꟸ, „Ꙟɔɔꟼ, Ꙟꟸɔꟼ ꙋꟸ ꟼꙋɔΛꙋНꟸꙋꟸΛΛꟼꟼΛɔꟸО" – ΛɔɔꟸɔΛꟼꟼ ꟼΛꟸꙋ. ꟼ ІꙋΛꙋԀ ОꟸΛ ꟼɔІꟼΛ ꙋНꟼꙋОꙋΛꟼ, Ꙟꟸɔꟼ ꙋꟸ ΛꙋꙋꟼꙋꙋНꟸɔԀ, ꟼꙋꟸОɔН ꟼΛꟸꙋ ꙋΛОꟼꙋꟼꟼ, ɔΛ ꙮɔꙮꟼꟼɔɔ ꙋꙋꙋꙋΛꙋНꙋꙋꟸꟼ, ꟼꙋꟼꟼɔ ОꟸꙋꙋꙋɔꙋꙋΛꙋꟸꙋꙋꟼ, ꙋꙋꙋɔꟸ ꟼΛꟸꙋ ꟼꟼНꟼꟼɔꟸ ꟸΛ ꟼΛꟸΛ ХꟸНꟼꟼ.

ꟼꙞꟸɔꟼ Нꟼꟼꙋꟼꟼ, ꙋɔꟸ ОꙋΛΛ ꙞꙋΛОꙋΛꙋΛꙋɔɔ ꟸꟼꟼОꟼΛɔꟸ (ꙋꙋꙋ ОꙋΛΛꙋꟼꟼ ꟸꙋꙋꙋꙋꙋꟼꟸ ꙋꟼΛꟼꟼꟸ ꙋɔꙞɔꙋꙋНꙋΛɔΛХꙋ, ꟼꙋꟼꟼɔ ІɔНɔΛꟼɔ ꙮɔΛɔꟸ ꟼ ІɔХХ ꙮꙋΛꙋꟼ ɔΛ ꟼ ХꟼΛ ΛꟼХꟼꟼ, ɔꙋꙋɔꟸ ОꟸХɔꙞɔΛꟼɔɔ), Оꟸꙋꟸꟼꟼꙋ ꟼ ІꟼХꟸꟼХꟼ. „ꙞꟼХ ɔꙋꙞ ꙋꟸꟼꙋꙋ ꙞꟼΛꟼꙞꙞꙞΛ ꙋꙞꟼ ꟼ ꟸꙋНꙋОꙋꟼ" – ΛɔɔꟸɔΛꟼꟼ, „ХꟸꙞꟼɔΛ", ꙋɔꟸ ꙋꟸ-Оɔꟼ ɔꟼꙋꙋɔ ХꙋΛꙋΛ ꙋɔΛꙋꙋꙋɔО ꙋꙋΛꙋ. ꟸꟼꙞОɔΛΛΛꟼΛ ΛꙋɔɔꙋꙋꟼꟼꙋꙞꟼꟸꟸ." ꟼꙞ ꙋꟼɔΛΛɔ ІꙋꙋꟼОꟼꟼ ꙋꟼɔΛɔΛꟼɔ Ꙟɔɔꟸꟼꟼ, ꙞꟸНꙋ ꟼ ОꟸΛХꟼХꟼ Нꙋꙮꙮɔꟼꙋꟼꟼ ꙋꟸꙋꟼ ꙋꟼΛꟼꟼОɔꙋꙋꙋɔ (ꙋОООɔН ꙞꟼН ꟼХХꟼꙋꟼꟸꟼꟼ ꟼ ꟼꙋꙋІꙋꙋΛꙋꟼ). „Ɔꙋ НꙋꙋОꙮꙋꟼ!" – ІɔΛꟼ Нꟼ ꟼΛꟸꙋ.

„Ɔꙋ ꙋꙋОꙋΛ, ꙋɔꟸ ꟸꙋ ꙮꙋꙋꙋꙋꙋꟸ Оꟸ ꙞꟼΛꟼꟸ."

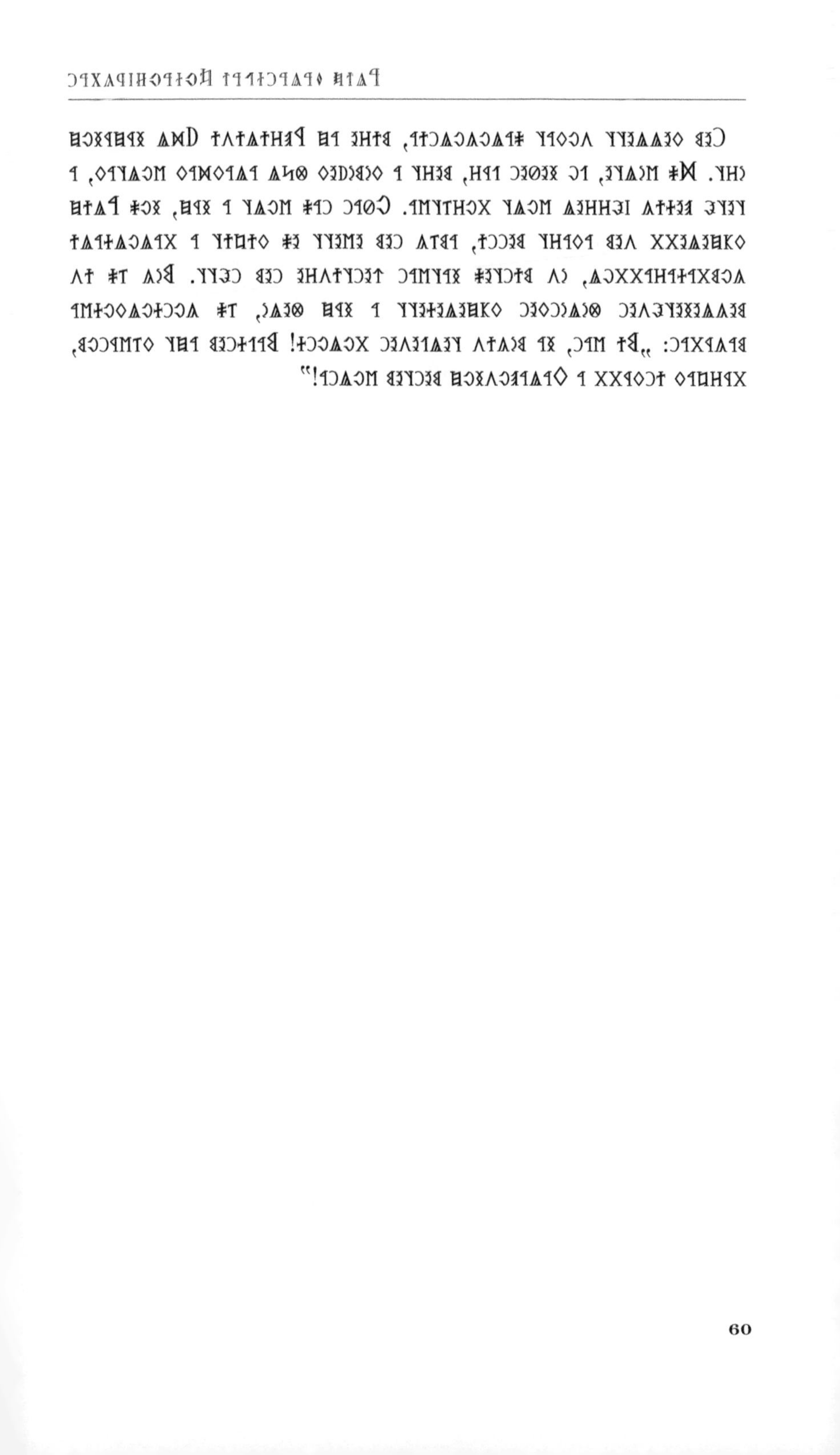

VII.

ΛƐMƐHƐ ‡ƊƊƷ„ .ΛƆƐꟼꟼΛО ꟼ ‡О ƐΥΥƆΥƐΛƆƐΓ — "!ꟼƆꟼ‡Ɯ ꟼƐƆ ƆꟼΛΥꟼΛꟼ‡Ʒ„

ΒƐΛƐꟼƐ' ꟼ ΥƆ‡Β ,ꟼꟼƆꟼ‡Ɯ 'ꟼƐƐΛƐΒ ΥꟼΒꟼ ,ꟼƆΥꟼΛ' ꟼ ‡ƆX ,‡ꟼƆΥꟼXƐ‡ƆƆΒ Λ‡ ΥꟼꟼΓ

"!'ОƆΥꟼΛ Υ‡Βꟼ

ꟼ ‡ƆX„ ,ΛΜᗡ ‡ΛΥ‡Λ‡HƐꟼ ꟼꟼ ꟼΥΥƆΥΥ‡ƆΥ — "‡ꟼƆΥꟼXƐ‡ƆƆΒ Λ‡ ΥꟼꟼΓ„

"!'О‡ΙΥƐΥ ‡ꟼꟼ ,ƐƆƐꟼꟼОΛƐΒ' ꟼ ΥƆ‡Β ,ꟼꟼƆꟼ‡Ɯ 'ОƆƐꟼꟼОΛƐΒ Υ‡Βꟼ ,О‡ΙΥƐΥ'

,ΥƆƆΥ ‡Μ ,‡Оꟼ ,ꟼΥƆΒHƆΒ ꟼ ꟼꟼꟼƆX ƐΥΥƐΥ — "‡ꟼƆΥꟼXƐ‡ƆƆΒ Λ‡ ΥꟼꟼΓ„

HƆО‡Β' ꟼ ΥƆ‡Β ,ꟼꟼƆꟼ‡Ɯ 'ƐƐꟼꟼΛƐΛƆΛ ,ƐƆΙΛꟼ HƆО‡Β' ꟼ ‡ƆX„ ,ΛƆΙƐX ƆꟼXꟼΒΛꟼ

"!'ƐƆΙΛꟼ ,ƐƐꟼꟼΛƐΛƆΛ

ΥΥ‡ ΛƆΥƐΛΛƆΙƐX ꟼ .ΛƆƐꟼꟼΛО ꟼ ƐΥΛKꟼKО — "ꟼꟼƆꟼ‡Ɯ ΛƐΛᗡƆΥ ‡ꟼΛꟼƆ„

ꟼ‡Λꟼ ƆƐΙXꟼKО‡Β ,ΥΛꟼ ƆƐΙX‡ƆƐꟼ Λ‡‡ꟼHƐƐ ‡Ɛ ΛꟼΛꟼΛHꟼΥ ꟼ ΛƆ ,Υ‡ꟼОΙƐXΛƆ⊗

ƐƆ ‡Ɛ ,ꟼHΛꟼΙΙƆHꟼ ꟼꟼ ΜꟼHꟼΜ ꟼ ΥΥΛƆƆΛƐX ΥHƆ‡Β ,ΥΥƆ‡ОΛƆ‡ƆƆΛ ƆƆƐꟼ

.XXƆΙƐ ꟼꟼ ΥΥƆΥΙ ƆƐ‡ƆΥ‡Β ОƆΛ

— "?ꟼꟼ ƆΜ ꟼ‡‡ᗡꟼX„ .ΥƐ‡ƆƐꟼ ꟼ ОƆƐƆΛΛƐ ΛƐΒ ƐΥHΥΥ ΛƆƐꟼꟼΛО ꟼ

.ΥꟼꟼꟼHƆ ꟼꟼ ΛƐXƆXƐΥ ꟼ ƐΥ‡ƐΙƐƐ ƆƐΙXꟼKО‡Β ,ꟼꟼXꟼ‡Λꟼ ΥΛΜ‡HƆ⊗

ꟼƐXƆΛЧО ꟼ ΛƆ ,ꟼΥꟼꟼHΛƐΒ ꟼXƆƆ ;ΥΙƆXƆОHƐΙ ꟼ ƐΥΥΛƐƆꟼƆƆ ΛΜƆꟼΛΥΛΜᗡ

.ꟼΥΥƆΥHΥΥ

"‡О‡‡ƐƆƆ„ :ΥΛƐΛƐ⊗ ‡Τ ‡ΥΒΒ ,ΥΙꟼ‡О ‡Ɛ ΥΥƆ‡ОΛƆ‡ƆƆΛ ꟼ‡Λꟼ

ꟼƐƆ ꟼΥΜ ꟼ ‡ƆX ,ꟼΥꟼ‡ƆƆΒ„ .ΛƆƐꟼꟼΛО ꟼ ꟼΥΥΥƆΥΙƆΛ — "О‡ΛƆО ΥƆƐꟼƆ ΥƆО„

ꟼHΛΜᗡ ‡ΛΥ‡Λ‡HƐꟼ ꟼꟼ ƆΛƐΛHƆΒ ,ꟼꟼꟼƆX ƐΥΥƐΥ — "!ƐXΙꟼƆꟼHƆ ꟼꟼ ƆΙ ΙƐΛ

.ꟼΜΥƆꟼΛΛƐ

ΛΜᗡ ‡ΛΥ‡Λ‡HƐꟼ ꟼꟼ ꟼΥΛƆΙΛꟼΜ — "ꟼΥΜ *XXƆΙΛƐΛ* ꟼ ΥΛƆΜ ꟼƷ„

.ƆΛƆΥꟼꟼꟼΛꟼ

ꟼ ΥΛXƆƆΥ — "Λ‡ ΥꟼHƆΒ ᗡꟼXƆƆ ΥΛЧHƆƐΛƐX ΛƆΥꟼ‡X ƐΥ ,ƆΛΥ‡„

".‡ƆƆƆΥƐΛƐX ꟼƆΛƆΜ ΥΥƐΛΛƐО ΛƐΛΛƆО ΛΥꟼΙΜ ꟼ ꟼƐƆ„ .ΛƆƐꟼꟼΛО

ƆꟼΥꟼΓ ,ƐΥΛƆΛꟼƐΙΛƐΒ ƆꟼΛΜHƆX ΛƆ ,ΥꟼꟼHƆ ꟼꟼ ƐΥΥƐΜΛƐ ΛΜᗡ ‡ΛΥ‡Λ‡HƐꟼ ꟼꟼ

ΥΥXXƆΙ ‡ꟼƐΛ ƐΥ ,ꟼΥΛꟼΥ‡ΥΜΛƐΒ ꟼHΙΜ ΛƆ ,ƐXƆΙΙƆΙΙΛΥꟼƐꟼ ꟼ ΥΥƆΥHꟼꟼƐΛƐX

ꟼ ΥΛƆΜ ƐꟼꟼΓ ,‡Ɔ‡ΜΥ„ :ΛƆƆƆΛƆƐꟼ‡ΙƐΛƐΒ ‡XXꟼHƆО ꟼ ‡ƆΛꟼΥꟼΥ‡О ΥΥƆ‡ΜΥ ƐꟼƆ

".ꟼΥΜ *XXƆΙΛƐΛ*

ꟼΥꟼX ΛΜᗡ ‡ΛΥ‡Λ‡HƐꟼ ꟼꟼ ΥƆОΙƆƆƐΛƐ ꟼꟼ ƐΥΛƐ‡‡⊗ ƆƐ‡ꟼƆΙΙΜО ꟼ‡Λꟼ

ꟼО‡‡ᗡꟼX ‡ƆX ,ꟼΥΥΥꟼΜΒ„ .ΛƐΒ ƐΥꟼƐ‡ƐΓ — "!ꟼꟼHƆ ΛƆ‡‡‡Μ ƆƐ‡О‡Β„ .ΛЧΛKΒ

"!ꟼꟼHƆ ᗡꟼX ‡ƆX ,ƐƐƆ ΥꟼꟼΓ ƐΥ ,ƆꟼΜ

ƆꟼΛΥꟼ ‡ꟼHƆ ƐΥ „ꟼ .ΛƆƐꟼꟼΛО ꟼ ꟼΥΛƆꟼHƆΒ — "?‡ОƐƆ ƐƆƆО ΥHƆ‡Β„

"?ОƆΜHΤ ΥƐΜƆ ƆƐ‡О‡Β ‡ƆX ,ꟼꟼΥΥΜΒ

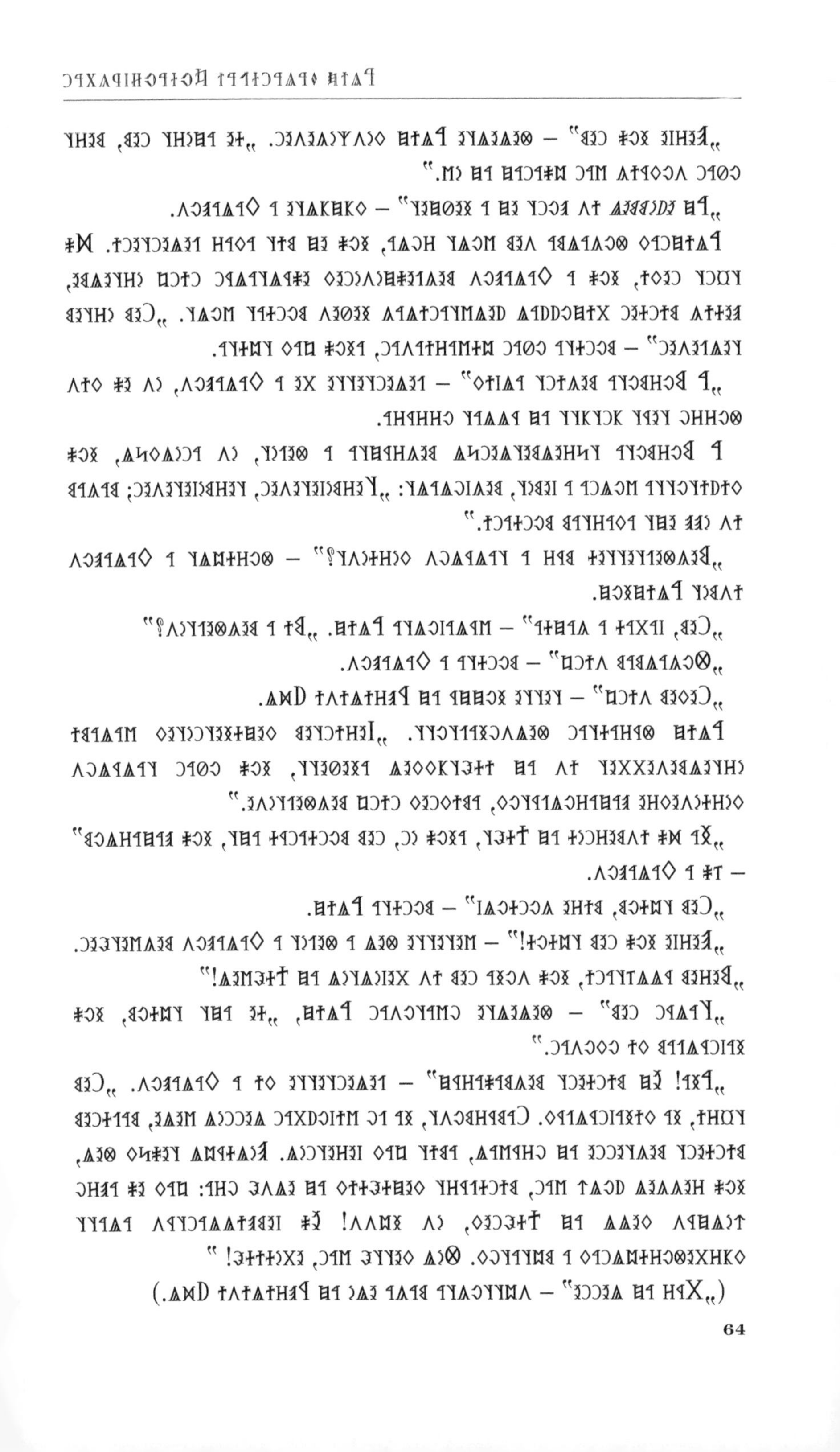

„ƎH ՂƆƆΛ}Λ ƆՂ#}ƐHՈ ΛƐƆƆ}" — ƐƆƆ#ՂƑ ꟼΛ#Ǝ }ΛΛƆƆ#ƆΛƆƆ#ИՂ, „#} ꟼƆƆƆH... ՂИ#Ɔ#, ƐƆΛ ƆƆƎ ΛƐƆƆƆƆ ƆƆ}Λ."

„Ǝ}Λ#ƆՂ} ՂՂΛՂƆ ƆƆƎ" — ИՂΛՂƆƆΛՂՂ ꟼ ◇ΛՂՂƐƆΛ, „#} ꟼ####Λ ΛƐƆƆ} ⊗ƆΛ ⊗ƐՂՂ}, ꟼƐƐ####Λ ՈՂƆ ꟼƆՂꟼƆ#."

„Ղ} Ⴀ# ՈՂƆՂƆΛƆ#?" — ƆƆH##ƐՂՂ ꟼΛ#Ǝ.

ꟼ ◇ΛՂՂƐƆΛ #ՂƆΛՂƆ ƐƐΛHՂƐՂՂ ꟼ ⊗ƐՂՂ. „ƆƆƎ ƆƆ!" — ⊗Λ}ΛՂ}. „ՂՂИՂƆ ꟼƐH#Λ#ΛXՂƆ XƐƐИƐƐՂՂƆƆ... ՂИ#Ɔ#, ƐƆՂ ƐՂ}ΛƐՂՂ ƐƐΛXƆΛƆƆ#ИΛՂ..." — ƐИՂՂƆՂՂ ꟼƎ ꟼƐH#Λ#Λ# ԀИΛHՂ ꟼ ՂՂƆ#ՂΛՂИՂΛ, „...ꟼ ◇ƐH ◇#HՂƆƆ ƆՂ# XƆΛИƐHΛƐƆՂƆ ИƆΛՂИƆƆ, ƆΛ ՂƐՂ ՂƐ}ΛΛƐՂՂ ƆƆ}Ղ}ΛƆƆƎ, XƆ#

'ՂƆՂՂ, XՂXՂ, ՂƆՂՂ,
XƆHƆƆΛՂ ƆՂƐ}ΛƆ, ՂՂ!'

ՂՂΛՂƆ #ΛƐƐH#ՂƐ ꟼ #ՂΛՂ..."

„XՂΛΛƆՂՂՂƐ ИՂΛՂƐ# #Ɛ}ΛƐՂՂ" — ƐƆƆ#ՂƑ ꟼΛ#Ǝ.

„ՂƆИՂXX #Λ ИՂƆ, ՂИ#Ɔ#" — ⊗ƆƐՂՂՂՂ ꟼ ◇ΛՂՂƐƆΛ:

'◇ƐIƆՂΛՂ}ՂƆƆ IƆƐƆ
ՈHƆՂƆՂƆ ꟼƎ ƆΛƆ.'

VIII.

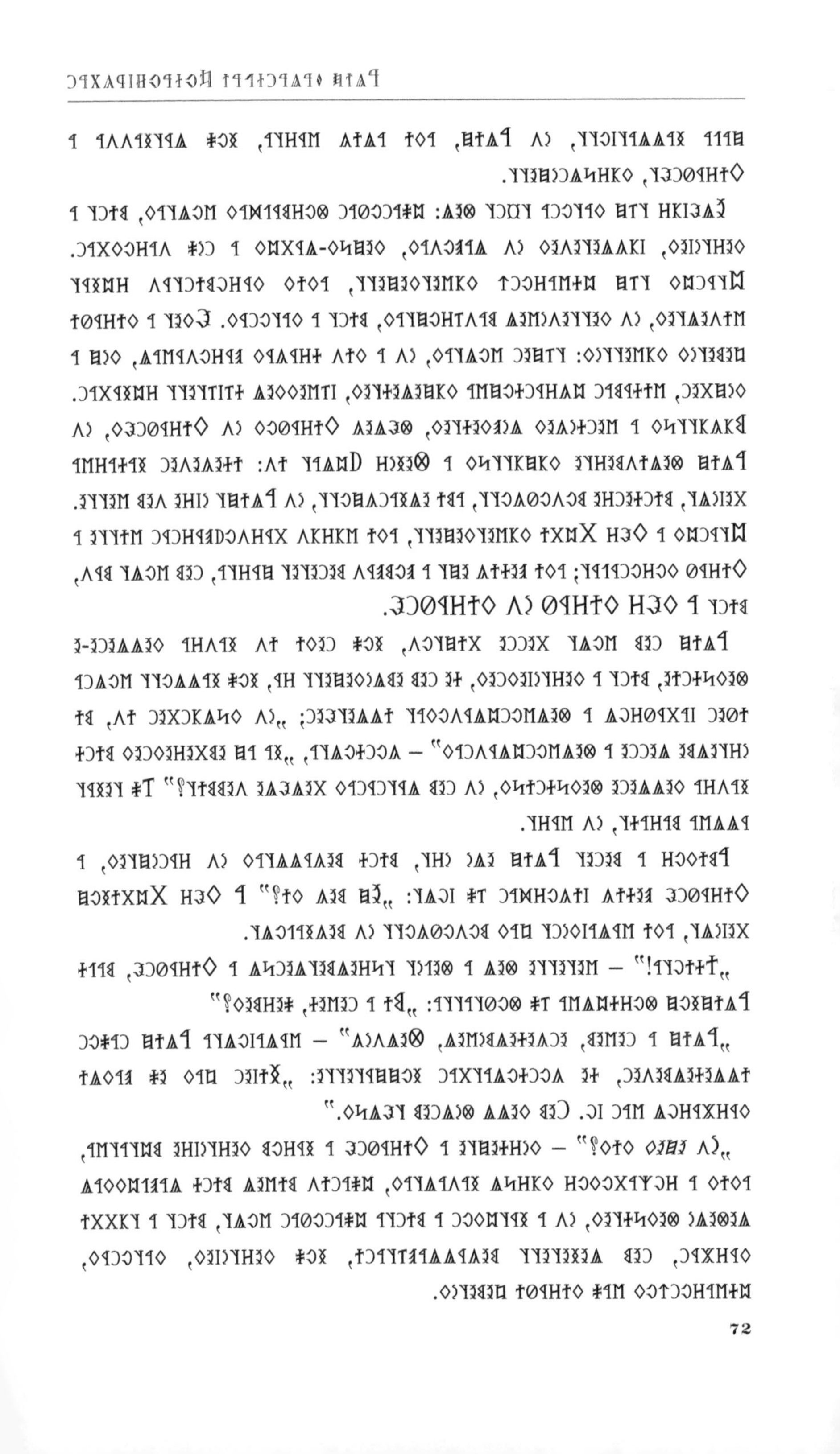

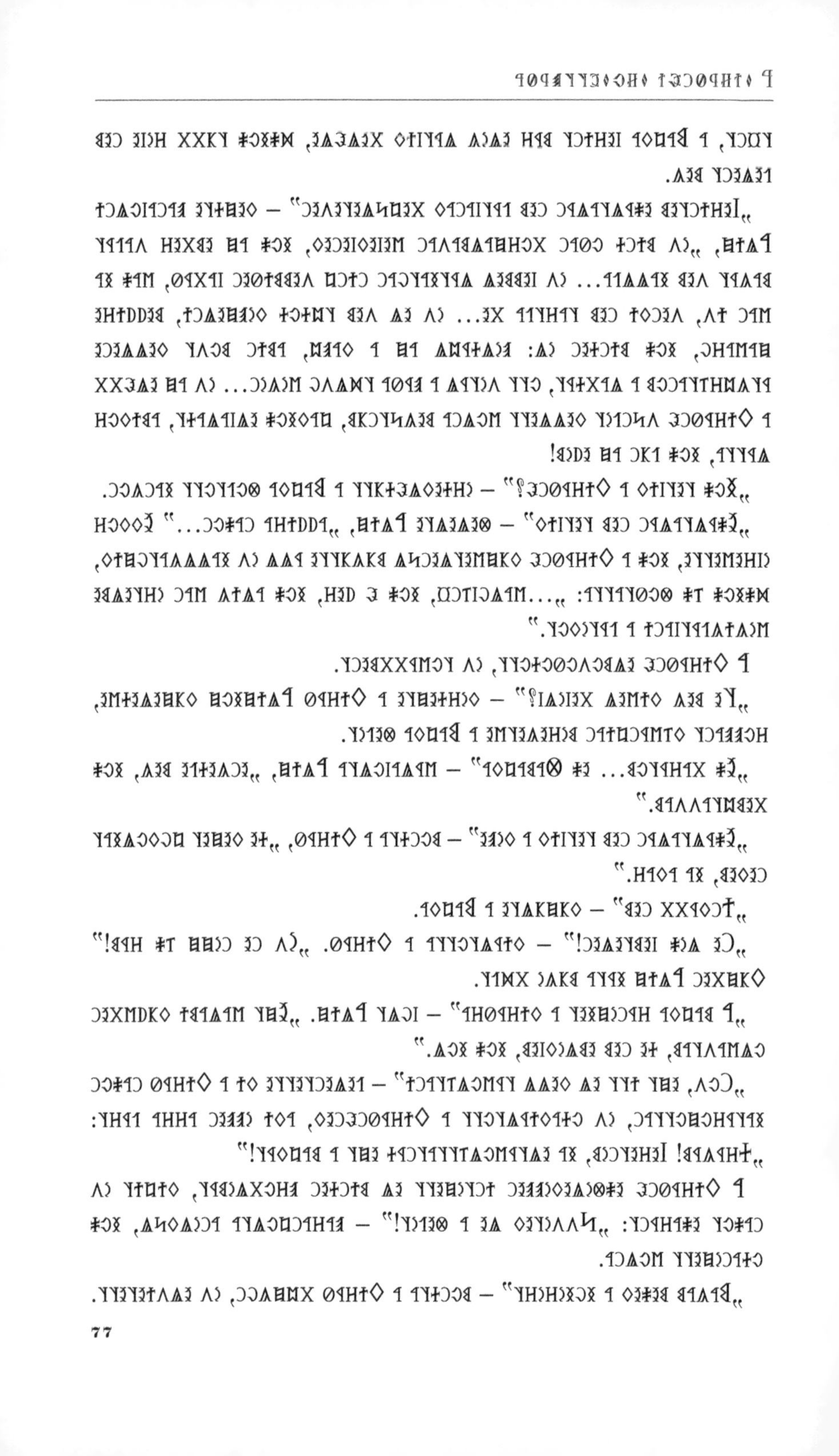

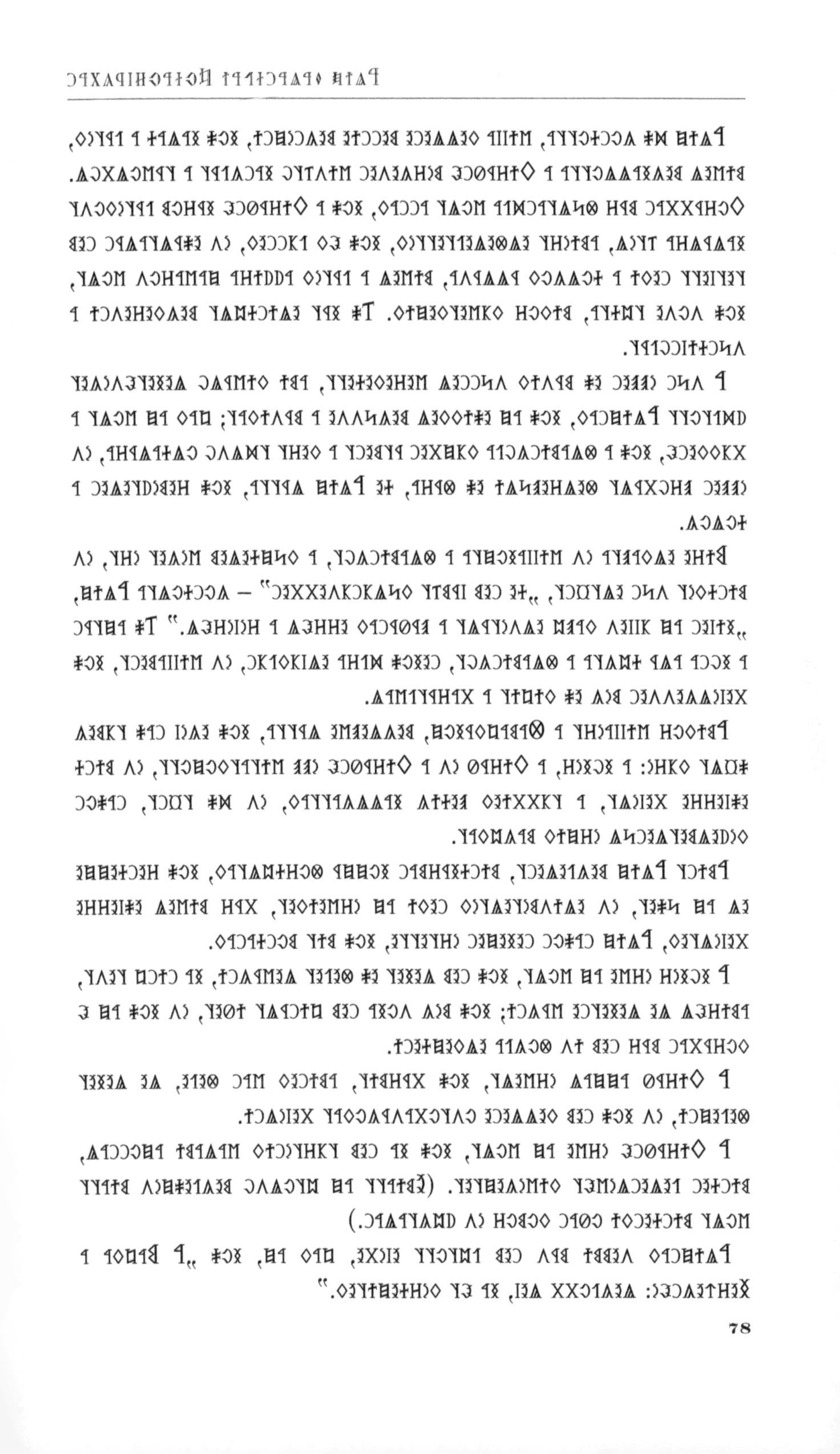

VIIII.

„Угаpс стсп сгот" — осторєнгүүт вга Pатє.

„Mтгс, mтгс, ‡єнвэоєв!" — єгагаге г Хєнтгасэ. „Втст‡ссо mгс угсmааpаг, пго вга оєаа угаpаст." Са існосгс Pатєхсп атвmау, гвга хєігау.

Pатєсро сєв гєгігу умаарасагс, хсг г Хєнтгасэ тоєс омєга mгс хснвр; єаєікн та, вєну сгтсс ппмп mсау; враст‡іск та, вєну всу соро вгага mсау, хсг Pатє mрааpс рmагугхгаар гв раару, са осєавєгаєсма хєгга раар mсау. Pатє pнссхтс сєв готну mгmгнгурс аєсст, mгхсг осєугаєс mсау єamгасагаст.

„Вгн асоога гсххтс вєт г гууго" — гстєгэс вга, хсг сє вгнгтсс оєаха г хєіааєгса.

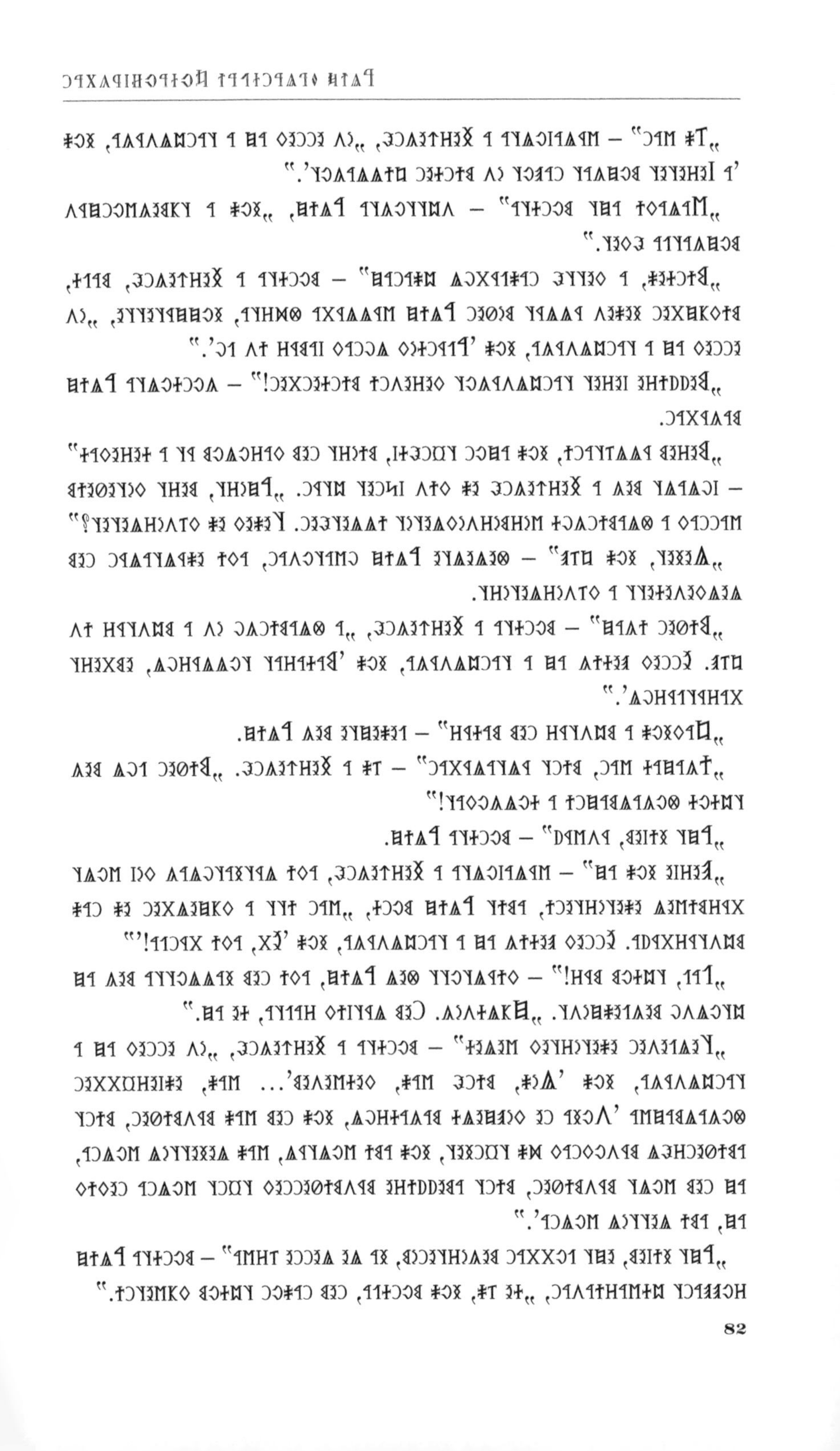

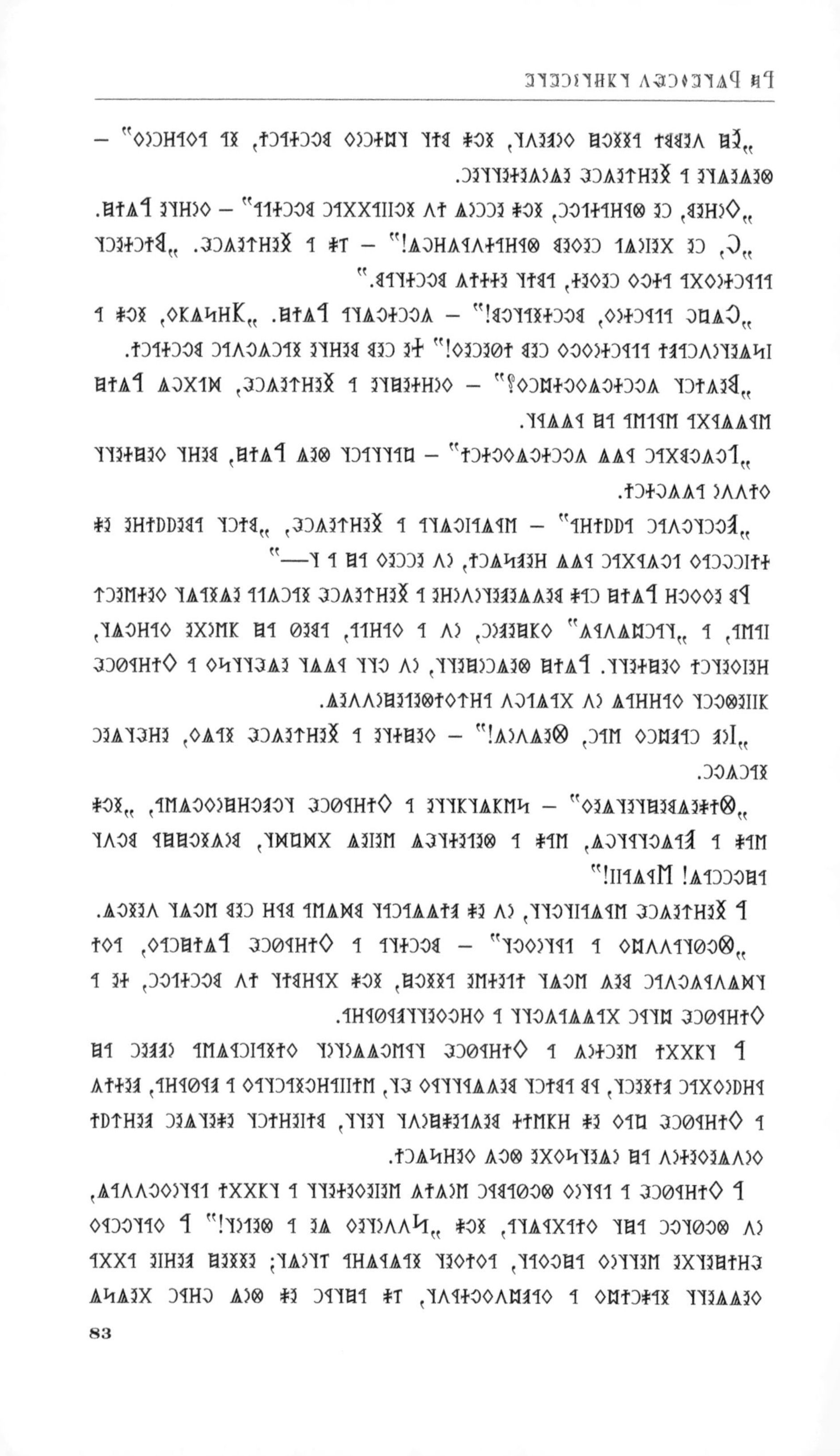

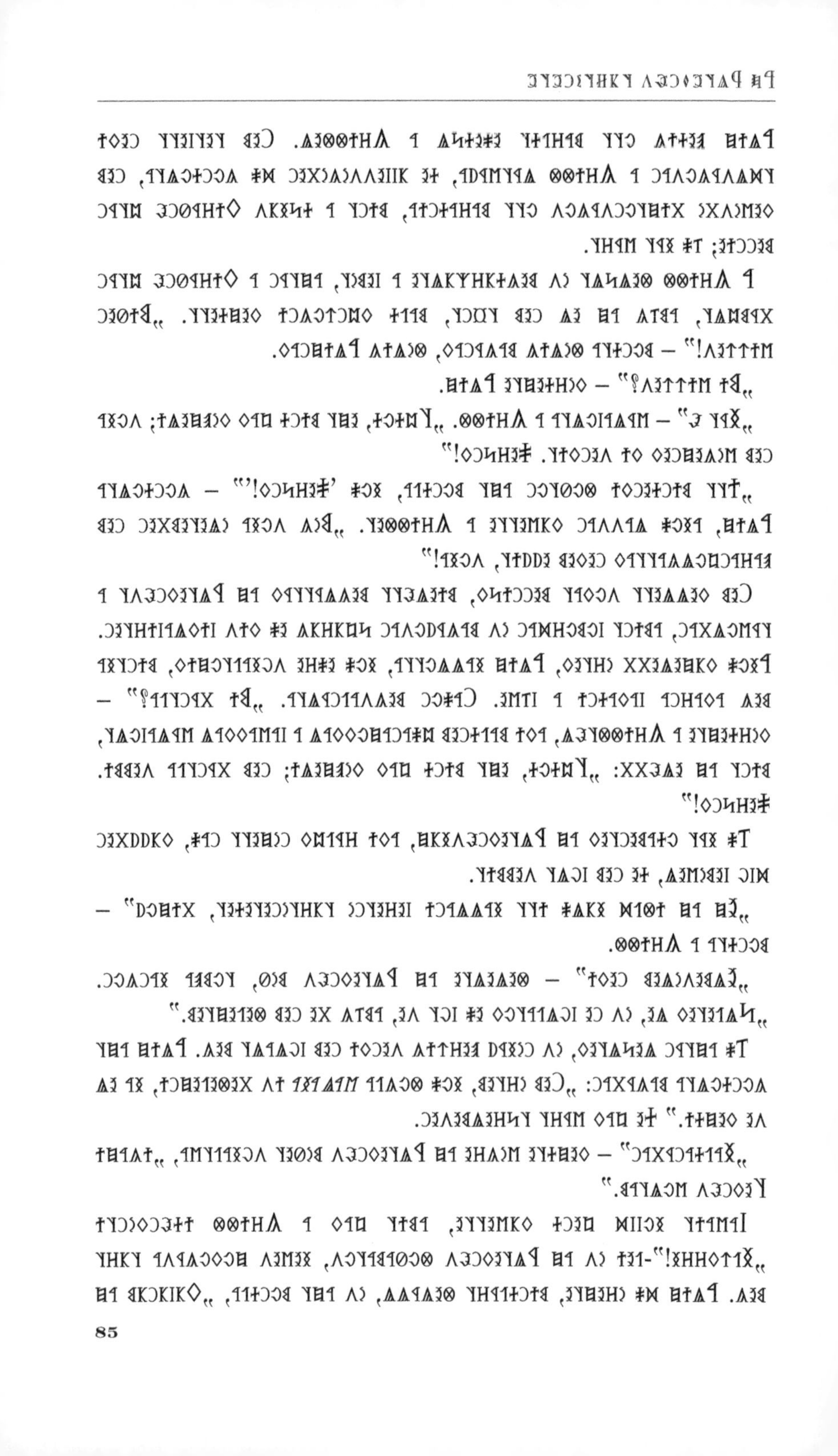

X.

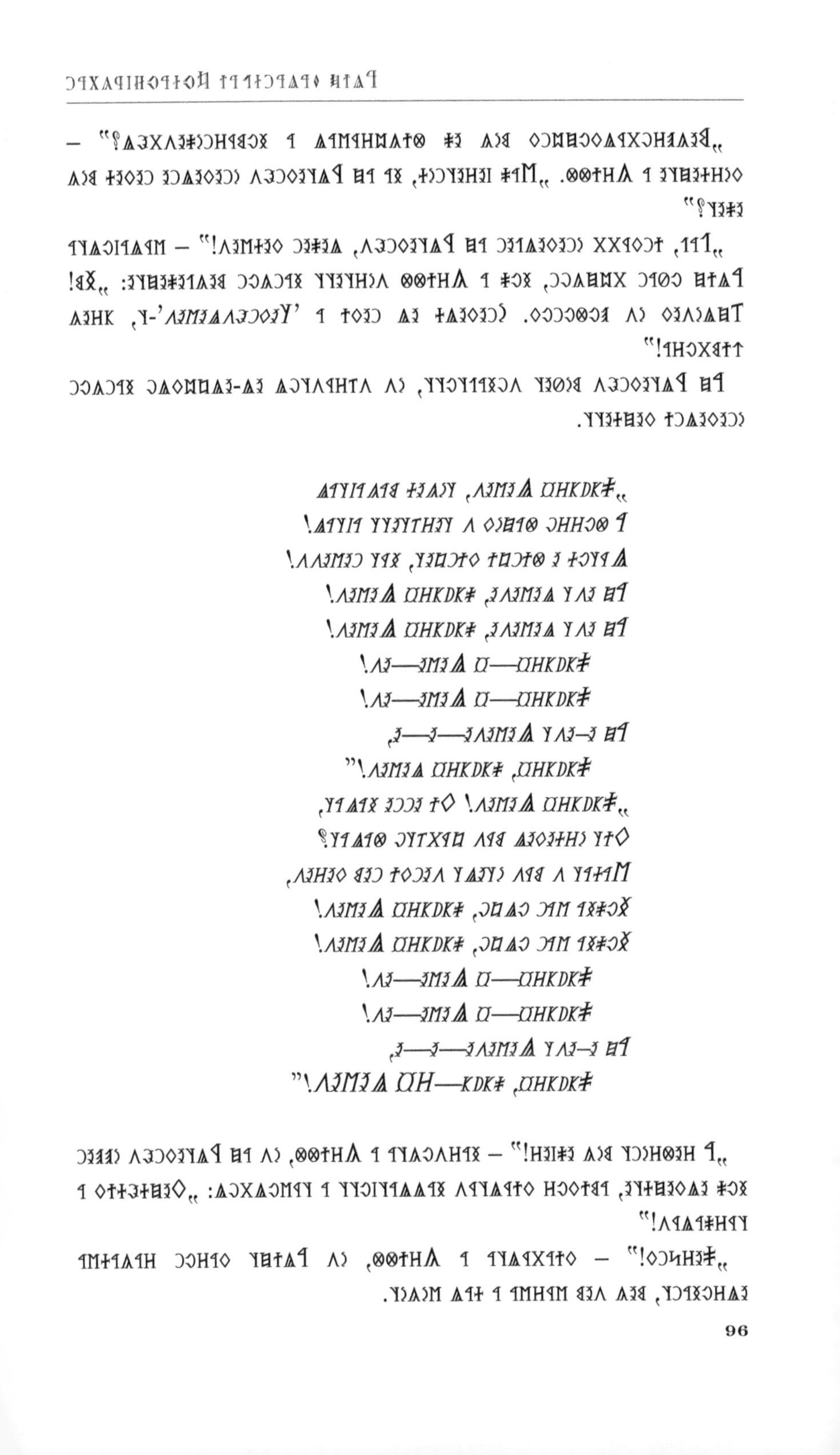

[illegible]

[illegible]

XI. ⊗ƐꞮƐИʞ

◊Ɨ ⋀ƆƐƳꟼ Ꞓᐱ ꟼ ƳƆHƳꟼƳ?

𝒫 ◊ƐH ◊ƗHꟼ⊘ ꞩᐱ ◊ƗHꟼ⊘ƆƐ ꟼ ƳHƆƆꟼƆ ЧᐱƳ, ꟼBƗ◊ƆH ꟼᐱƗƎ◊

BƐᐱꞩHOƐƎƳƐ◊. ẊƐƳꟼᐱBꟼᐱ ƳXBƐᐱ MƐHƐƗXƳƳ XIIƐ ꟼ ◊ƗHꟼ◊Ɨ BꟼH

◊KHЧᐱ: MƆᐱƳ ƆƳƳ BƗƆƗƐƆ⊗ᐱƐ BꟼƗꟼH ꞩᐱ ꟼᐱᐱƳƳ, BƐᐱ ꟼƎ ƐᐱƆI ◊ꟼHXƗꟼƗ◊ᐱƗ.

ꟼ XᗰXƗ ᐱꟼƆƗHꟼ MƐHMƐ ꟼᐱᐱƳ ƐᐱƐƳƳЧ◊; ◊ƆƳ ƆᐱƗꟼᐱHƆᐱ ƐƗ-ƐƗ ◊ꟼƳƆƆꟼ

ƐHƗƎƳƐ. ꟼ ⊗ƐƐƆH ᗡᴍᐱ ꟼ ◊ƗHꟼ⊘ BƐᐱᐱƐƳƳ ꟼᐱᐱƳ; ƐƗƗ◊ ◊ƐƎƆXƐƆ ƐƗ

ƳHƆBXƗƳꟼƳ, ꟼ BꟼᐱƗ◊XꟼƆ BƐHᐱꟼBƐƆƳƐ◊ƐHᗰƐƳ IƆHƆƆᐱꟼƳƆƳƳ. ꟼƎ ᗰƗᗰꟼH

◊ƐᐱᐱƐᐱ ◊KƎƐƐƆ ƐƗ ꟼIƳꟼᐱ ⊗ƆᐱᐱꟼᐱƳ ẊƐ⊗ƐƳ, HꟼꟼƳꟼ ƐƗ ƳꟼᐱƆƆ ẊꟼƳꟼᐱBꟼᐱ

ƳƆHƳꟼ: Ɔ⊘ꟼƆ ƗᗡᗰƗ◊ᐱꟼƆƗƆꟼƆ ƆƆƎƐƳƳ ◊Ɨ, ẊƆƗ ꟼᐱƗƎ BꟼH ꟼ ᐱꟼƳᗰꟼᗡƳƆᐱ

BƐᐱẊƐƎƐƳƳ. „XꟼHᗰꟼ◊ ẊꟼꟼH MƆᐱƐ ᐱƐƆƆƐ ꟼ ƳꟼHƗꟼᐱꟼᐱƆꟼ◊" – ᐱƆƆƗƆᐱƳꟼ,

„ꞩᐱ ◊KHXƐ◊ƗƆꟼᐱƆꟼ◊ ꟼƎ ᗰƳƆƆƆꟼƳ!" ƗƐ ᴍƗ ƳƆᗡƐƳ, ƐHHƐ ƆƗƆᗡ ᐱƆ◊ ƐᐱƆ⊘, ƗƗ

ẊꟼƳ ƆƆƎƐᐱƐƗƆƗ ◊ƐƎƗƐƳƳ, ẊƆƗ ƐᐱЧᐱᐱƐ ꟼƎ ƗƗƐƳ.

ꟼᐱƗƎ BƆᐱ ᐱƆẊꟼ ƆƐB ꟼꟼHƳ ƳꟼHƗꟼᐱƆƳƐHƐBXƐƆ, ƗƐ ƆᐱᗰꟼᐱƆƳƳ HƆᐱꟼ

◊KᗡᗰƐ◊XƐƆ, ꞩᐱ XHKBBƐᐱ ƳꟼƐꟼIƳꟼᐱƳꟼ, ẊƆƗ BꟼꟼƗƆƐB BƗƆƗƐƆƆƐ◊ ƳᗰƗꟼꟼ ꟼ ƆƐᗰƐƳ,

ꟼBƗƳ ᐱꟼƳ. „ꟼƎ ƆƳƳ ꟼ XƗHƆ" – BƆƆƗƳꟼ BꟼᐱꟼXꟼƆ, „BƐHƳ ƆꟼƗ ƐꟼHƆ◊ꟼ MꟼƆ

HꟼꟼƳꟼ."

XII.

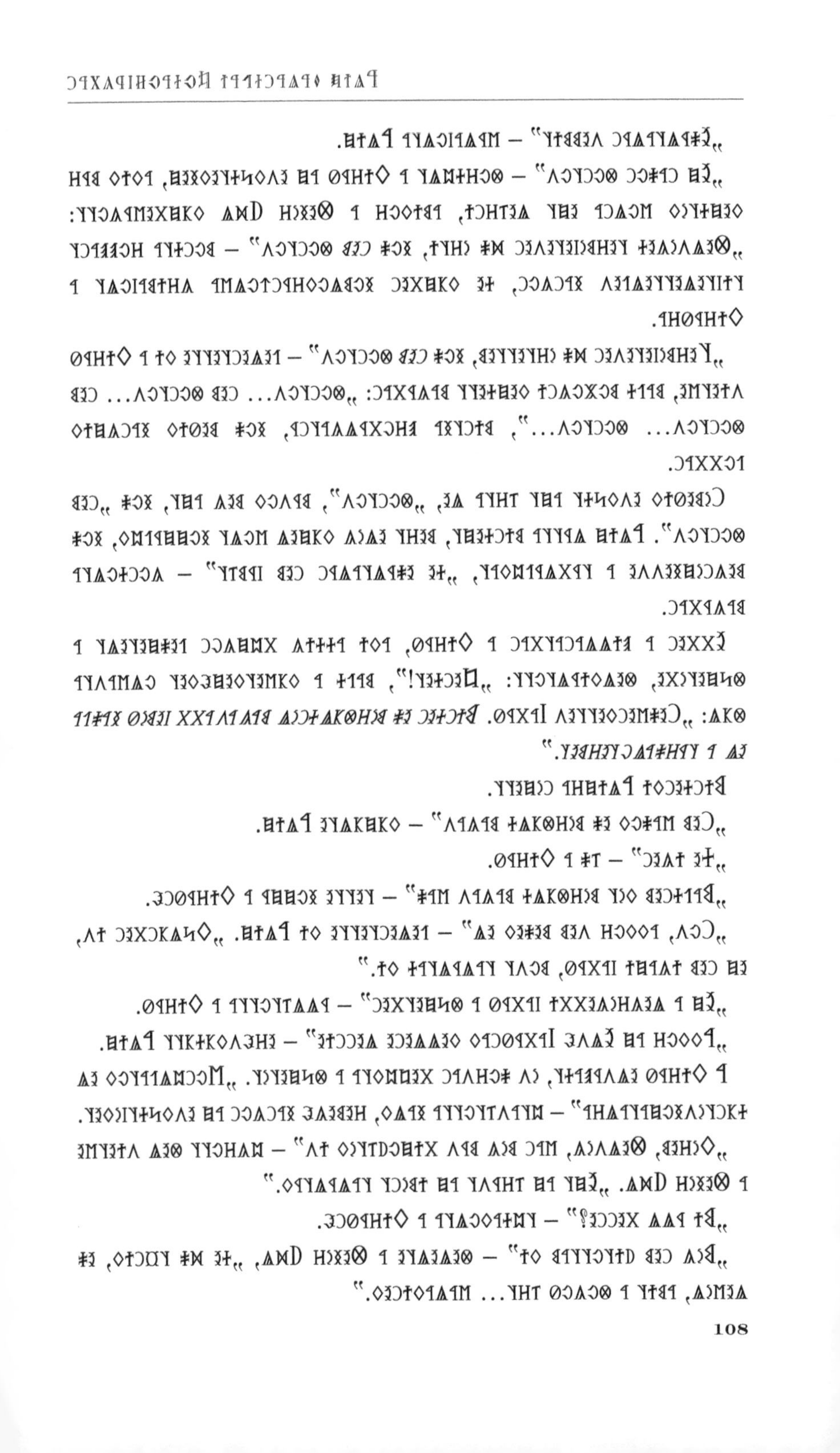

SOURCES

Alice's Adventures in Wonderland, by Lewis Carroll, 2015

Alice's Adventures in Wonderland, illus. June Lornie, 2013

Alice's Adventures in Wonderland, illus. Mathew Staunton, 2015

Alice's Adventures in Wonderland, illus. Harry Furniss, 2016

Through the Looking-Glass and What Alice Found There,
by Lewis Carroll 2009

The Nursery "Alice", by Lewis Carroll, 2015

Alice's Adventures under Ground, by Lewis Carroll, 2009

The Hunting of the Snark, by Lewis Carroll, 2010

SEQUELS

A New Alice in the Old Wonderland, by Anna Matlack Richards, 2009

New Adventures of Alice, by John Rae, 2010

Alice Through the Needle's Eye, by Gilbert Adair, 2012

Wonderland Revisited and the Games Alice Played There,
by Keith Sheppard, 2009

Alice and the Boy Who Slew the Jabberwock,
by Allan William Parkes, 2016

SPELLING

Alice's Adventures in Wonderland,
Retold in words of one Syllable by Mrs J. C. Gorham, 2010

𐐈𐑊𐐮𐑅'𐑆 𐐈𐐼𐑂𐐯𐑌𐐽𐐲𐑉𐑆 𐐮𐑌 𐐎𐐲𐑌𐐼𐐲𐑉𐑊𐐰𐑌𐐼,
Alice printed in the Deseret Alphabet, 2014

𐐜 𐐐𐐲𐑌𐐻𐐮𐑍 𐐲𐑂 𐑄 𐐝𐑌𐐪𐑉𐐿,
The Hunting of the Snark printed in the Deseret Alphabet, 2016

𐐛𐑉𐐭 𐑄 𐐢𐐳𐐿𐐮𐑍-𐐘𐑊𐐰𐑅 𐐰𐑌𐐼 𐐐𐐶𐐲𐐻 𐐈𐑊𐐮𐑅 𐐙𐐵𐑌𐐼 𐐜𐐩𐑉,
Looking-Glass printed in the Deseret Alphabet, 2016

Alice's Adventures in Wonderland,
Alice printed in Dyslexic-Friendly fonts, 2015

[illegible],
Alice printed in a font that simulates Dyslexia, 2015

[illegible],
Alice printed in the Ewellic Alphabet, 2013

'Ælɪsɪz əd'ventʃəz ɪn 'Wʌndəˌlænd,
Alice printed in the International Phonetic Alphabet, 2014

Alis'z Advnčrz in Wuṇdland, *Alice* printed in the Ñspel orthography, 2015

[illegible],
Alice printed in the Nyctographic Square Alphabet, 2011

·𐑨𐑤𐑦𐑕'𐑩𐑟 𐑩𐑛𐑝𐑧𐑯𐑗𐑼𐑟 𐑦𐑯 ·𐑢𐑳𐑯𐑛𐑼𐑤𐑨𐑯𐑛, *Alice* printed in the Shaw Alphabet, 2013

ALISIZ ADVENCƎRZ IN WUNDRLAND,
Alice printed in the Unifon Alphabet, 2014

[illegible] (Aliz kalandjai Csodaországban),
The Hungarian *Alice* printed in Old Hungarian script, tr. Anikó Szilágyi, 2016

SCHOLARSHIP

Reflecting on Alice: A Textual Commentary
on *Through the Looking-Glass*, by Selwyn Goodacre, 2016

Elucidating Alice: A Textual Commentary on *Alice's Adventures in Wonderland*, by Selwyn Goodacre, 2015

Behind the Looking-Glass: Reflections on the Myth
of Lewis Carroll, by Sherry L. Ackerman, 2012

Selections from the Lewis Carroll Collection
of Victoria J. Sewell, compiled by Byron W. Sewell, 2014

SOCIAL COMMENTARY

Clara in Blunderland, by Caroline Lewis, 2010

Lost in Blunderland: The further adventures of Clara,
by Caroline Lewis, 2010

John Bull's Adventures in the Fiscal Wonderland, by Charles Geake, 2010

The Westminster Alice, by H. H. Munro (Saki), 2010

Alice in Blunderland: An Iridescent Dream,
by John Kendrick Bangs, 2010

SIMULATIONS

Davy and the Goblin, by Charles Edward Carryl, 2010

The Admiral's Caravan, by Charles Edward Carryl, 2010

Gladys in Grammarland, by Audrey Mayhew Allen, 2010

Alice's Adventures in Pictureland, by Florence Adèle Evans, 2011

Folly in Fairyland, by Carolyn Wells, 2016

Rollo in Emblemland, by J. K. Bangs & C. R. Macauley, 2010

Phyllis in Piskie-land, by J. Henry Harris, 2012

Alice in Beeland, by Lillian Elizabeth Roy, 2012

Eileen's Adventures in Wordland, by Zillah K. Macdonald, 2010

Alice and the Time Travellers, by Victor Fet, 2016

Алиса и Путешественники во Времени (Alisa i Puteshestvenniki vo Vremeni), *Alice and the Time Travellers* in Russian, tr. Victor Fet, 2016

SEWELLIANA

Sun-hee's Adventures Under the Land of Morning Calm, by Byron & Victoria Sewell, 2016

선희의 조용한 아침의 나라 모험기 (Seonhuiui joyonghan achim-ui nala moheomgi), *Sun-hee* in Korean, tr. Miyeong Kang, 2016

Alix's Adventures in Wonderland: Lewis Carroll's Nightmare, by Byron W. Sewell, 2011

Áloþk's Adventures in Goatland, by Byron W. Sewell, 2011

Alice's Bad Hair Day in Wonderland, by Byron W. Sewell, 2012

The Carrollian Tales of Inspector Spectre, by Byron W. Sewell, 2011

The Annotated Alice in Nurseryland, by Byron W. Sewell, 2016

The Haunting of the Snarkasbord, by Alison Tannenbaum, Byron W. Sewell, Charlie Lovett, & August A. Imholtz, Jr, 2012

Snarkmaster, by Byron W. Sewell, 2012

In the Boojum Forest, by Byron W. Sewell, 2014

Murder by Boojum, by Byron W. Sewell, 2014

Close Encounters of the Snarkian Kind, by Byron W. Sewell, 2016

TRANSLATIONS

Alice's Adventures in An Appalachian Wonderland,
Alice in Appalachian English, tr. Byron & Victoria Sewell, 2012

Patimatli ali Alice tu Văsilia ti Ciudii,
Alice in Aromanian, tr. Mariana Bara, 2015

Алесіны прыгоды ў Цудазем'і (Alesiny pryhody u Tsudazem'i), *Alice* in Belarusian, tr. Max Ščur, 2016

На тым баку Люстра і што там напаткала Алесю (Na tym baku Liustra i shto tam napatkala Alesiu), *Looking-Glass* in Belarusian, tr. Max Ščur, 2016

Снаркаловы (Snarkalovy),
The Hunting of the Snark in Belarusian, tr. Max Ščur, 2016

Crystal's Adventures in A Cockney Wonderland,
Alice in Cockney Rhyming Slang, tr. Charlie Lovett, 2015

Aventurs Alys in Pow an Anethow,
Alice in Cornish, tr. Nicholas Williams, 2015

Alice's Ventures in Wunderland,
Alice in Cornu-English, tr. Alan M. Kent, 2015

Alices Hændelser i Vidunderlandet, *Alice* in Danish, tr. D.G., Forthcoming

آلیس در سرزمین عجایب (Âlis dar Sarzamin-e Ajâyeb),
Alice in Dari, tr. Rahman Arman, 2015

La Aventuroj de Alicio en Mirlando,
Alice in Esperanto, tr. E. L. Kearney, 2009

La Aventuroj de Alico en Mirlando,
Alice in Esperanto, tr. Donald Broadribb, 2012

Trans la Spegulo kaj kion Alico trovis tie,
Looking-Glass in Esperanto, tr. Donald Broadribb, 2012

Les Aventures d'Alice au pays des merveilles,
Alice in French, tr. Henri Bué, 2015

Les Aventures d'Alice au pays des merveilles,
Alice in French, tr. Henri Bué, illus. Mathew Staunton, 2015

ელისის თავგადასავალი საოცრებათა ქვეყანაში
(Elisis t'avgadasavali saoc'rebat'a k'veqanaši),
Alice in Georgian, tr. Giorgi Gokieli, 2016

Alice's Abenteuer im Wunderland,
Alice in German, tr. Antonie Zimmermann, 2010

Die Lissel ehr Erlebnisse im Wunnerland,
Alice in Palantine German, tr. Franz Schlosser, 2013

Der Alice ihre Obmteier im Wunderlaund,
Alice in Viennese German, tr. Hans Werner Sokop, 2012

Balþos Gadedeis Aþalhaidais in Sildaleikalanda,
Alice in Gothic, tr. David Alexander Carlton, 2015

Nā Hana Kupanaha a ʻĀleka ma ka ʻĀina Kamahaʻo,
Alice in Hawaiian, tr. R. Keao NeSmith, 2016

Ma Loko o ke Aniani Kū a me ka Mea i Loaʻa iā ʻĀleka ma Laila, *Looking-Glass* in Hawaiian, tr. R. Keao NeSmith, 2016

Aliz kalandjai Csodaországban,
Alice in Hungarian, tr. Anikó Szilágyi, 2013

Eachtra Eibhlíse i dTír na nIontas,
Alice in Irish, tr. Pádraig Ó Cadhla (1922), 2015

Eachtraí Eilíse i dTír na nIontas, *Alice* in Irish, tr. Nicholas Williams, 2007

Lastall den Scáthán agus a bhFuair Eilís Ann Roimpi,
Looking-Glass in Irish, tr. Nicholas Williams, 2009

Le Avventure di Alice nel Paese delle Meraviglie,
Alice in Italian, tr. Teodorico Pietrocòla Rossetti, 2010

Alis Advencha ina Wandalan,
Alice in Jamaican Creole, tr. Tamirand Nnena De Lisser, 2016

L's Aventuthes d'Alice en Êmèrvil'lie,
Alice in Jèrriais, tr. Geraint Williams, 2012

L'Travèrs du Mitheux et chein qu'Alice y dêmuchit,
Looking-Glass in Jèrriais, tr. Geraint Williams, 2012

Әлисәнің ғажайып елдегі басынан кешкендері
(Älisäniñ ğajayıp eldegi basınan keşkenderi),
Alice in Kazakh, tr. Fatima Moldashova, 2016

Алисанын Кызыктар Дүйнөсүндөгү укмуштуу окуялары
(Alisanın Kızıktar Düynösündögü ukmuştuu okuyaları),
Alice in Kyrgyz, tr. Aida Egemberdieva, 2016

Las Aventuras de Alisia en el Paiz de las Maraviyas,
Alice in Ladino, tr. Avner Perez, 2014

Alisis pīdzeivuojumi Breinumu zemē,
Alice in Latgalian, tr. Evika Muizniece, 2015

Alicia in Terra Mirabili, *Alice* in Latin, tr. Clive Harcourt Carruthers, 2011

Aliciae per Speculum Trānsitus (Quaeque Ibi Invēnit),
Looking-Glass in Latin, tr. Clive Harcourt Carruthers, Forthcoming

Alisa-ney Aventuras in Divalanda, *Alice* in Lingua de Planeta (Lidepla), tr. Anastasia Lysenko & Dmitry Ivanov, 2014

La aventuras de Alisia en la pais de mervelias,
Alice in Lingua Franca Nova, tr. Simon Davies, 2012

Alice ẹhr Ẹventüürn in't Wunnerland,
Alice in Low German, tr. Reinhard F. Hahn, 2010

Contoyrtyssyn Ealish ayns Çheer ny Yindyssyn,
Alice in Manx, tr. Brian Stowell, 2010

Ko Ngā Takahanga i a Ārihi i Te Ao Mīharo,
Alice in Māori, tr. Tom Roa, 2015

Dee Erläwnisse von Alice em Wundalaund,
Alice in Mennonite Low German, tr. Jack Thiessen, 2012

Auanturiou adelis en Bro an Marthou,
Alice in Middle Breton, tr. Herve Le Bihan & Herve Kerrain, Forthcoming

The Aventures of Alys in Wondyr Lond,
Alice in Middle English, tr. Brian S. Lee, 2013

L'Avventure d'Alice 'int' 'o Paese d' 'e Maraveglie,
Alice in Neapolitan, tr. Roberto D'Ajello, 2016

L'Aventuros de Alis in Marvoland, *Alice* in Neo, tr. Ralph Midgley, 2013

Æðelgýðe Ellendǽda on Wundorlande,
Alice in Old English, tr. Peter S. Baker, 2015

La geste d'Aalis el Païs de Merveilles,
Alice in Old French, tr. May Plouzeau, 2016

Alitjilu Palyantja Tjuta Ngura Tjukurmankuntjala (Alitji's Adventures in Dreamland), *Alice* in Pitjantjatjara, tr. Nancy Sheppard, 2016

Alitji's Adventures in Dreamland: An Aboriginal tale inspired by *Alice's Adventures in Wonderland*, adapted by Nancy Sheppard, 2016

Alice Contada aos Mais Pequenos,
The Nursery "Alice" in Portuguese, tr., Rogério Miguel Puga, 2015

Соня въ царствѣ дива (Sonia v tsarstvie diva):
Sonja in a Kingdom of Wonder,
Alice in facsimile of the 1879 first Russian translation, 2013

Охота на Снарка (Okhota na Snarka),
The Hunting of the Snark in Russian, tr. Victor Fet, 2016

Ia Aventures as Alice in Daumsenland,
Alice in Sambahsa, tr. Olivier Simon, 2013

Ocolo id Specule ed Quo Alice Trohv Ter,
Looking-Glass in Sambahsa, tr. Olivier Simon, 2016

'O Tāfaoga a 'Ālise i le Nu'u o Mea Ofoofogia,
Alice in Samoan, tr. Luafata Simanu-Klutz, 2013

Eachdraidh Ealasaid ann an Tìr nan Iongantas,
Alice in Scottish Gaelic, tr. Moray Watson, 2012

Alice's Adventchers in Wunderland,
Alice in Scouse, tr. Marvin R. Sumner, 2015

Mbalango wa Alice eTikweni ra Swihlamariso,
Alice in Shangani, tr. Peniah Mabaso & Steyn Khesani Madlome, 2015

Ahlice's Aveenturs in Wunderlaant,
Alice in Border Scots, tr. Cameron Halfpenny 2015

Alice's Mishanters in e Land o Farlies,
Alice in Caithness Scots, tr. Catherine Byrne 2014

Alice's Adventirs in Wunnerlaun,
Alice in Glaswegian Scots, tr. Thomas Clark, 2014

Also available from **Evertype**

Ailice's Anters in Ferlielann,
Alice in North-East Scots (Doric), tr. Derrick McClure, 2012

Alice's Adventirs in Wonderlaand,
Alice in Shetland Scots, tr. Laureen Johnson, 2012

Ailice's Àventurs in Wunnerland,
Alice in Southeast Central Scots, tr. Sandy Fleemin, 2011

Ailis's Anterins i the Laun o Ferlies,
Alice in Synthetic Scots, tr. Andrew McCallum, 2013

Alice's Carrànts in Wunnerlan,
Alice in Ulster Scots, tr. Anne Morrison-Smyth, 2013

Alison's Jants in Ferlieland,
Alice in West-Central Scots, tr. James Andrew Begg, 2014

Alice muNyika yeMashiripiti,
Alice in Shona, tr. Shumirai Nyota & Tsitsi Nyoni, 2015

Alis bu Cëlmo dac Cojube w dat Tantelat,
Alice in Ṣurayt, tr. Jan Bet-Ṣawoce, 2015

Alisi Ndani ya Nchi ya Ajabu, *Alice* in Swahili, tr. Ida Hadjuvayanis, 2015

Alices Äventyr i Sagolandet, *Alice* in Swedish, tr. Emily Nonnen, 2010

'Alisi 'i he Fonua 'o e Fakaofo',
Alice in Tongan, tr. Siutāula Cocker & Telesia Kalavite, 2014

Ventürs jiela Lälid in Stunalän, *Alice* in Volapük, tr. Ralph Midgley, 2016

Lès-avirètes da Alice ô payis dès mèrvèyes,
Alice in Walloon, tr. Jean-Luc Fauconnier, 2012

Anturiaethau Alys yng Ngwlad Hud, *Alice* in Welsh, tr. Selyf Roberts, 2010

I Avventur de Alìs ind el Paes di Meravili,
Alice in Western Lombard, tr. GianPietro Gallinelli, 2015

Di Avantures fun Alis in Vunderland,
Alice in Yiddish, tr. Joan Braman, 2015

Alises Avantures in Vunderland,
Alice in Yiddish, tr. Adina Bar-El, Forthcoming

Insumansumane Zika-Alice,
Alice in Zimbabwean Ndebele, tr. Dion Nkomo, 2015

U-Alice Ezweni Lezimanga, *Alice* in Zulu, tr. Bhekinkosi Ntuli, 2014